Junkers Ju 90

Karl-Heinz Regnat

MIDLAND
An imprint of
Ian Allan Publishing

Junkers Ju 90
© Bernard & Graefe Verlag, 2002, 2004

ISBN 1 85780 178 4

First published 2002 in Germany by
Bernard & Graefe Verlag, Bonn

Translation from original German text
by Ted Oliver

English language edition published 2004 by
Midland Publishing
4 Watling Drive, Hinckley, LE10 3EY, England
Tel: 01455 254 490   Fax: 01455 254 495
E-mail: midlandbooks@compuserve.com

Midland Publishing is an imprint of
Ian Allan Publishing Ltd

Worldwide distribution (except North America):
Midland Counties Publications
4 Watling Drive, Hinckley, LE10 3EY, England
Telephone: 01455 254 450   Fax: 01455 233 737
E-mail: midlandbooks@compuserve.com
www.midlandcountiessuperstore.com

North American trade distribution:
Specialty Press Publishers & Wholesalers Inc.
39966 Grand Avenue, North Branch, MN 55056
Tel: 651 277 1400   Fax: 651 277 1203
Toll free telephone: 800 895 4585
www.specialtypress.com

Design concept and layout
© 2004 Midland Publishing and
Russell Strong

Printed in England by
Ian Allan Printing Ltd
Riverdene Business Park, Molesey Road,
Hersham, Surrey, KT12 4RG

Contents

The Progenitors

Prof. Dr.-Ing. Hugo Junkers: The Life and Tragedy of a Genius

Before examining one of the most significant Junkers aircraft not to be designed under the leadership of Hugo Junkers, it is appropriate to give a brief portrayal of his life, his work, and the unworthy fate that was imposed upon him by a regime contemptuous of human life – a fatal development in his later years that led to his sudden downfall and death.

The third child of Heinrich and Luise Junkers, Hugo Junkers was born on 3rd February 1859. The family was expanded by five more children in succeeding years to a total of seven boys and one girl; the sole daughter, however, died while still a small child. Since 1650 the Junkers family had been rooted in the small town of Rheydt in the Rheinland, and it was here that Heinrich Junkers, following the family tradition, established a weaving firm. The family suffered a heavy blow when their mother passed away in 1869, when Hugo was only ten years old, and the majority of his brothers even younger. Hugo's education is summarised as follows:

- Attended the Kinderverwahrschule (Children's Repository School) in Rheydt
- Preparatory School for Gymnasialausbildung (Grammar or Secondary School Education)
- 1867-74: Höhere Bürgerschule (Higher Citizens' School)
- 1875-78: Gewerbeschule (Trade or Business School) in Barmen
- From 1878: various Hochschulen (Colleges or Universities) in Berlin, Karlsruhe and Aachen. It was here in the summer of 1883 that Hugo Junkers completed his Regierungs-Maschinenbauführer (Government Mechanical Engineering Manager) examinations, and could now apply that title to himself.

Having completed his studies, he spent several years with various companies as a designer. It was during this period that his father met with a tragic fate on 17th November 1887 as a result of gas poisoning. In the following year, now aged 29, Hugo became associated with Wilhelm Oechelhaeuser in Dessau, and an important stage in his life was the founding of Versuchsstation für Gasmotoren (Experimental Station for Gas Motors) von Oechelhaeuser & Junkers, which the two men built up together. Finances came from the legacy of Hugo's father, but by 1890 the two partners had gone their separate ways.

In terms of research work, Hugo Junkers wanted a free hand, and he now devoted himself intensively to research. In 1892 he founded his own firm in Dessau and applied for patents in the field of Wärmetechnik (Heat Technology). Five years later he took up a Professorial Chair in Thermodynamics at the Technische Hochschule in Aachen, in addition to which he headed the Engineering Laboratory. In 1912 he terminated his activities there. During this period he married his wife Theresa, and between the years 1899 to 1920 they had no fewer than 12 children.

During the course of his research work, the Junkers-Gegenkolben-Zweitakt-Schwerölmotor (opposed-piston two-stroke diesel engine) appeared, which had considerable potential in providing power for trucks and buses through to giant powerplants for ships and industrial installations. In 1913 Hugo founded the Junkers Motorenwerke in Dessau, but the plant was closed in 1915 as a result of his activities in the field of the metal construction of aircraft, on which he now concentrated (with the foundation of the Research Institute, Dessau).

His first contact with aviation and the ongoing quest to conquer the third dimension had come in 1908 through one of his colleagues at the TH Aachen, Prof. Hans Reissner, who had concerned himself for a number of years with the theoretical and practical problems of flight. On the basis of relatively little aeronautical technical knowledge, the renowned canard called the Reissner Ente had made its appearance, with which Reissner successfully accomplished a few flights that were more in the nature of aerial 'hops'. The Professor's endeavours provided the 'initial spark' for Hugo Junkers, who began to concentrate his efforts in this new realm; as early as 3rd December 1909 he had drawn up a patent proposal for a tailless aircraft – a Junkers vision for an enormous long-range civil aircraft capable of accommodating more than 100 passengers. It was clear to him, however, that this seemingly utopian proposal under the conditions existing at that time could only be achieved in stages. Now 50 years of age, Junkers would be unable to realise this dream in the form envisaged.

Prof. Dr.-Ing. Hugo Junkers (3rd February 1859 to 3rd February 1935).

In the meantime the dark clouds of war had formed on the horizon, which, in August 1914, would billow into a World War lasting four years – and a war fought in a dimension that until then humanity had not experienced. Due to the call-up of several of his employees, Hugo's development of his large engines soon came to a standstill, and he now turned his attention to even more intensive research in the field of aviation. He recognised the revolutionary value of the aircraft as a weapon even before numerous officers of the Army High Command, who had grown up in the sphere of two-dimensional warfare. This shortsightedness of the military mind, moving along conventional lines, caused not inconsiderable difficulties for the work of Junkers and others, who were occupied with the subject. Not only that, although he enjoyed a superb reputation in other spheres of activity, in the sphere of aviation his competence was largely a matter of dispute. Junkers was not a pilot, nor could he provide proof of a specific aeronautically-oriented education. His unconventional design principles were a further hindrance, which could only be grasped with difficulty, or not at all, by those accustomed to

thinking solely in terms of wood, canvas and steel tubing. The fact was that Junkers was not an expert in this field, and therefore did not attract support in the form of experimental contracts. This opinion, held by those in responsible positions, condemned Hugo Junkers to self-financing his further research in the field of all-metal aircraft. Of course, he himself was completely convinced of his ideas on the subject, and the future would confirm his conviction a thousandfold in the shape of the most diverse all-metal aircraft.

In 1915 the J 1 made its appearance, a single-seat fighter of all-metal construction covered with corrugated sheet metal – Junkers' 'trademark' and a particularly noticeable feature that would stretch like the proverbial 'red thread' through his aircraft over the next two decades. However, weight problems with the J 1, and the J 2 that followed, resulted in reduced manoeuvrability, and the all-metal aircraft almost came to an early end, but the situation was saved through the use of duraluminium, a revolutionary new material that reduced weight by two-thirds over the previously used iron sheeting, and provided a 20% increase in structural strength. One disadvantage was that, because of the lack of an aluminium welding method at the time, the panelling had to be fixed by rivets. In addition, new design forms had to be developed for this material, to which the manufacturing procedures had to conform. All these novelties were put into practice with the J 3 aircraft. The weight difference between the sheet-covered J 2 and the J 3 was one-third. Even before manufacture of the latter aircraft was completed, Junkers began to occupy himself intensively with the realisation of the J 4 infantry aircraft. As a result, the J 3 did not reach the completion stage and serve as the basis of experience thus far gathered until the J 7. Under the leadership of Dipl.-Ing. Otto Reuter and Prof. Dr.-Ing. Otto Mader, the J 4 'flying tank' – a heavy, armoured biplane of cantilever construction – accomplished its

maiden flight in January 1917, and was delivered to front-line units in July of that year. A total of 227 left the assembly lines, and they were well liked by their crews.

The J 5 and J 6 project studies likewise made their appearance during the First World War. The first was for a small, single-seat, low-winged monoplane fighter of duralumin construction. One of its particular features lay in its form of propulsion, whereby the force-cooled rotary engine was installed in the fuselage aft of the pilot, power from the engine being transmitted to the nose-mounted airscrew via an extension shaft. The single-seat parasol-winged J 6 fighter, dating from 1917, was not completed. Similar in appearance and calculated performance to the Fokker D.VIII, it would have provided a worthy competitor to the 'Royal Court Purveyor' fighter manufacturer Anthony Fokker. The cantilever high-winged aircraft was followed by the J 7, which represented a breakthrough into the low-winged type of light metal designs. The J 7 made its first flight on 18th September 1917, and during a series of trials that continued into the following year numerous alterations were made.

The J 8 and J 9 represented further fighter designs, after which came a state-ordered combination of two basically differing designs in the form of the Junkers-Fokker-Werke. This forced marriage, solemnised on 20 October 1917, brought together Hugo Junkers the scientist and the more practically-oriented Anthony Fokker, with the aim of achieving optimum results in the sphere of aircraft design, but neither Junkers nor Fokker was particularly interested in the joint effort. In May 1918 this young and short-lived enterprise received an initial order for the construction of 20 examples of the J 9, while Junkers was awarded contracts for the manufacture of the two-seat J 10 reconnaissance aircraft. From the J 10 was developed the J 11 reconnaissance floatplane, of which three examples were completed, representing the last Junkers-designed aircraft of the First World War.

In November 1918 'zero hour' chimed, and the production of aircraft, as well as other war materials, came to an abrupt end. The German aircraft industry – at least officially – almost ceased to exist, since between 1920 and 1922 the Treaty of Versailles totally forbade all activity in the aviation sphere. But even before this period, designers had started work on 'desk drawer' projects, and when the period had passed, weakly-motored aircraft were built for civil purposes; the payload limit for such aircraft was limited to 600kg (1,323 lb) and the service ceiling was not allowed to exceed 4,000m (13,120ft).

Junkers, meanwhile, had to release most of its 2,000 employees into an uncertain future. Hugo himself, during these years of turmoil, had never forgotten his dream of peaceful air travel that would bring citizens closer together, and just two months after the end of the war, in January 1919, an epoch-making civil aircraft began to take shape on the drawing-boards of the Junkers Research Institute. As early as 25th June 1919, this precursor of all the present-day turbojet-powered giants – the F 13 – made its maiden flight. The conditions necessary for civil aviation to blossom were certainly unthinkable in a Germany plagued with crises during this period, but undoubtedly the requisite amount of enthusiasm existed in several spheres. The country's circumstances, however, negated any large-scale plans, and Junkers could only expect success abroad. He therefore campaigned with success in the United States, and received a construction contract. Initially, a Mr Larson purchased a few F 13s and concluded a licence agreement with Junkers in 1919, enabling him to manufacture the aircraft in the USA. Several enterprises, among them SCADTA (Sociedad Colombo-Alemana De Transportes Aereos), established in 1919, flew routes in South America, mostly with aircraft from the Junkers stable. But the possibility also existed, as soon as favourable conditions presented themselves 'at the front door', so to speak, to sell Junkers products in Europe. The need for good-performance aircraft was doubtless considerable, since several destinations were being flown mainly with military aircraft that had been modified in a makeshift manner to satisfy civilian traffic requirements.

It was only when the manufacturing ban and the limitations imposed with it had been lifted that Junkers was able to participate in the development of air travel, which was expected to expand significantly in the coming years. At the same time, safety, reliability and, not least, punctuality of flight schedules increased in importance. Flying had advanced over the years from an adventure to more of a routine.

In 1922 Junkers established the Abteilung Luftverkehr (Air Traffic Department), and in the following year was occupied with an eleven-seater passenger aircraft – the G 24 – which made its appearance in 1925.

Under pressure of the Reich Government, Junkers now devoted itself to erecting a plant in Russia – in Fili, near Moscow – where Junkers aircraft would be built for the Soviets. In exchange, the latter permitted military aircraft to be tested that were still forbidden on German territory. However, as time passed the atmosphere between the Soviets and Germany cooled somewhat, with the result that Junkers had to withdraw its workforce. The costs involved stifled the firm's finances, and the threat of bankruptcy would only be averted if the Reich Government provided the appropriate reimbursements. The figure involved was no less than 20 million Reichsmarks, which the Government was only willing to pay as a result of a court judgement, otherwise Junkers would have been left 'in the cold'. Junkers had been able to satisfy its demands, but in doing so had made considerable enemies who were determined to pay Hugo back.

At the beginning of 1926 this precarious situation was used to coerce Junkers into relinquishing its airline, the Junkers Luftverkehr, and thus free the path for the establishment of a so-called Einheitsgesellschaft (unitarian company) in that year – a company now known as Deutsche Lufthansa, which originated out of the birth-pangs of the Junkers Luftverkehr and the previously state-subsidised Aero Lloyd airline.

Even when the scales, from an external viewpoint, appeared to have been balanced, the inclination of several official representatives was enmity towards Junkers, just waiting for a favourable moment to strike. Thus the seeds of intrigue were sown, and in the years to come would germinate, grow, and blossom. Only a few years remained to Junkers to devote his attention to his life's work, and during this period and under his leadership the following aircraft designs became a reality:

1924: G 23
1925: G 24, A 25, T 26, T 27, T 29
1926: K 30, G 31, A 32, A 35, W 33, W 34, R 42, K 53
1927: S 36, K 37, K 43
1928: K 47, A 48, A 50
1929: G 38, J 50
1930: K 47, Ju 52/1m
1931: Ju 49
1932: Ju 46, Ju 52/3m, Ju 60
1933: Ju 86 and Ju 89, initiation of development
1934: Ju 86 and Ju 160
          (already under Director Koppenberg)

The days of Hugo's unhindered creativity were now numbered. In November 1931 Junkers received a directive from the Working Group Sachsenberg to immediately put its finances in order. In the following month Hugo's son Klaus Junkers, together with Director August Mühlen, took over the leadership of the company, and in April 1932 Junkers Flugwerk Betriebs-GmbH was formed, governed by trustees, indicating that while Junkers-Werke was healthy from a salesmanship point of view, it had no liquidity. In order to generate funds, 'Jco' (Junkers & Co, which manufactured calorimeters and geysers) would be sold to Bosch AG. Events then moved rapidly. Only a few days after the Nazis came to at the helm, the RVM – Reichsverkehrsministerium (Reich Transport Ministry) – forced Prof. Hugo Junkers to hand over all the Junkers-Werke patents without financial compensation. Junkers at first refused, whereupon Hermann Göring and Erhard Milch brought their 'big guns' into play. This took place through the medium of Erich Lämmler, at the time one of the numerous state-sanctioned legal attorney manipulators. This State Prosecutor threatened Junkers that, should he not conform to the demand to hand over the patents, he would be put on trial as a traitor. After a series of strong verbal protests, Junkers recognised the futility of his situation and affixed his signature. Despite this, Lämmler still submitted a proposal to his superior to approve legal proceedings for state treachery. This, however, was rejected.

In September 1933 Junkers was confronted with yet another infamous demand, concerning the transfer of 51% of his shares in the Junkers-Werke to the RLM or Reichsluftfahrtministerium (German Air Ministry), the successor to the RVM; this was not only an impudent but also certainly a criminal demand, which Junkers, despite vehement opposition, could not overcome. Once again the increasingly broken manufacturer signed. On 24th November 1933 he was informed that Director Dr. Heinrich Koppenberg would henceforth assume his functions. Koppenberg now not only became the Company Head but also became Chairman of the Board, and Junkers was no longer permitted to even enter his own enterprise! Only a relatively small sum was paid to him, and, dispossessed and a broken man, Junkers left Dessau and withdrew to Gauting near Munich, where he devoted his energies to the development of ready-made houses of metal construction. His 75th birthday on 3rd February 1934 was celebrated by a small circle in Bayrischzell, where he lived under house arrest, and visitors were only permitted under police supervision. On that very day new demands were handed over to Junkers that would place further limitations on his short life ahead.

In September 1934 he underwent a serious operation, but hardly had he begun to recover when he fell seriously ill again due to new aggravations, and passed away on the day his 76th birthday. Hermann Göring and his cohorts had achieved their end. Hugo Junkers was buried six days later, on 9th February 1935; in a display of what was then the customary hypocrisy and shamelessness, he was given a state funeral. With extreme bad taste, the second highest man in the Nazi hierarchy, Rudolf Hess, offered with crocodile tears in his eyes his condolences to Hugo's widow.

The tragedy was compounded by a humiliating letter – naturally anonymous – that made the rounds, being distributed to various newspaper editors. The libels it contained had originated in September 1926, questioning all previous inventions and achievements and grinding the name of Junkers into the dirt. If Hugo Junkers lost his respectability, it could only be of benefit to his rivals, since he possessed the largest share of the land-based aircraft market. Dr.-Ing. Claudius Dornier, for example, whose metier was the floatplane, which sold well in both the military and civilian spheres, flew permanently in the shadow of the Dessauer. Unbelievable as it seems, it is a fact that Dornier was the author of these accusations. Details of this explosive topic are to be found in the book *Hugo Junkers* by Dr. Günter Schmitt (Aviatic Verlag, pp 257-259).

Hugo Junkers was undoubtedly a strong-willed individual with his own peculiar traits that made him hard to accept by many of his contemporaries. To cite his own evaluation of himself: 'I am a rugged fighter and I learned in the school of life to stand on my own feet and not depend on the benevolence of the large mass of humanity. I have long ceased to enquire what the majority of people think of me, especially when I am able to justify myself to my own satisfaction.'

The Junkers logo on the fin of the legendary W 33 *Bremen*.

Dipl.-Ing. Ernst Zindel: Aircraft Designer at Junkers

The life of one of the most significant German aircraft designers began on 23rd January 1897 when Ernst Zindel was born in Mistelbach in Oberfranken (Upper Franconia). At just 17 years of age he left the protective parental home and, in the general enthusiasm of the time, reported voluntarily for military service, which he spent in a Bavarian infantry regiment. He was severely wounded and, in 1916, following a long period of recuperation, he studied shipbuilding at the TH Charlottenburg. Four years later, Zindel arrived at Junkers, where he became a designer in Dessau. Hugo soon recognised the talent of this young man, and in 1922, following the death on 12th January of that year of his former leading engineer Dipl.-Ing. Otto Reuter, Zindel was appointed head of the Research Institute. Prof. Dr.-Ing. Otto Mader was his direct superior.

Ernst Zindel was now in charge of the design of the Junkers G 24, G 31, and the W 33/W 34 series of civil aircraft. Five years later, in 1927, Junkers appointed him head of the Development Department. In 1929-30 the giant G 38 followed, as well as the best-known Junkers aircraft among the general public, the legendary Ju 52. In 1932 Zindel took over responsibility for overall development as well as for

Dipl.-Ing. Ernst Zindel (23rd January 1897 to 10th October 1978), one of the best-known German aircraft designers.

flight-testing. During the next three years he climbed a few further steps up the career ladder in his capacity as Director of Design and Legal Deputy. Under his leadership, designs such as the Ju 87, Ju 88, Ju 90, Ju 290 and Ju 390 made their appearance, and up to the end of the Second World War Zindel was intensively occupied with various jet bomber projects.

Following the capitulation on 8th May 1945, Zindel's hitherto creatively rich years – at least in the sphere of aviation – were, like those of Junkers, a thing of the past. His future path did not lead him like numerous other colleagues to the United States or to the Soviet Union, but to Bad Homburg, where he was engaged on the design of stufenlose getriebe (stepless geared powerplants). He was also a guest university lecturer at the Technical Academy in Mühlheim on the Ruhr. When Ernst Zindel died on 10th October 1978, an undoubtedly satisfying professional life that had extended over more than 80 years came to an end.

The following is an extract from a lecture given by Zindel in 1938 on the principles of aircraft design and safety: 'Amongst all the world's aircraft companies that today manufacture aircraft for the civil sector, Junkers can point with complete certainty to the longest tradition and to the most diverse experience in this sphere. Junkers civilian transports have been flying for some 28 years to all parts of the world and have covered several million kilometres, often under the most difficult conditions with the greatest of reliability and safety.

'With the old, well-known Junkers F 13, the first real transport aircraft, Junkers had not only in 1919 established the basis for modern air traffic, but had also created the ideal and the basic construction for the modern, standard civilian air transport aircraft. Further development of the F 13 resulted in 1926 in several records and, through the trans-ocean flight of the aviator Hermann Köhl in the well-known W 33, also the W 34 – the first economic transport aircraft, which in subsequent years was employed with extraordinary success for postal and freight duties on both day and night services.

'Prior to this, however, in 1924, Junkers had made a further extremely significant and concrete step in the development of civil aviation in developing and putting into operation the first three-engined G 24 aircraft, designed to carry nine passengers and a crew of two.

'An increase in passenger frequency in the still young air travel at the time, coupled with the economic use of materials as well as flight and ground personnel and the requisite equipment needed for effective navigation, but above all for the necessary increase in flight safety and reliability with particular emphasis on passenger traffic, led us compulsorily at that time in this development direction to the three-engined large civilian transport aircraft. Not only was the German air traffic network established and expanded over most of Europe with this aircraft, but also that of large continental air traffic enterprises in a whole series of other European and non-European countries.

'The simplest and cheapest machine to evolve and operate is undoubtedly a single-engined one. It can without doubt be loaded up to the limit of its take-off capability insofar as its payload is not limited by minimum-altitude performance requirements. The machine will also undoubtedly be cheap in terms of maintenance, but when the engine fails, the aircraft is irretrievably forced to land as soon as possible. For this reason, the single-engined aircraft for modern air travel and particularly in bad weather conditions, falls completely out of the picture.

'The twin-engined aircraft, which can still maintain flight at a sufficient altitude, doubtless possesses a higher degree of flight safety. Its weak point is the eventual failure of one engine on take-off. In order, however, to achieve reliable flight safety with one engine, the aircraft should only have a moderate performance loading, but nevertheless has to be capable of flying at a sufficient altitude with less than 50% of the total power. In terms of its specific useful load, such an aircraft is economically less favourable. However, the twin-engined aircraft that is incapable of flying on only one engine, from the safety aspect is worse than a single-engined one and is therefore of no use for civil air traffic.

'A much more favourable compromise was and is, on the other hand, at least for medium ranges, the three-engined aircraft that is certainly capable of flight on two engines. Since it still has two-thirds of the power available in the event of the loss of one engine, it permits a higher useful load to be carried and with it a very good economic utilisation. In terms of flight safety, and powered by relatively reliable and tried-and-tested engines, it already provides a very high degree of reliability. The best proof of this is in the three-engined Ju 52 with its proven BMW engines, which, despite its many years of service and extraordinarily widespread use in air traffic operations, is not known to have suffered an emergency landing as a result of engine problems.'

Chapter One

Evolution

The Continual Development of Junkers Civil Aircraft

An Antecedent: The Reissner Ente

As a result of working of with his colleague Prof. Hans Reissner at the TH Aachen, Hugo Junkers developed an intensive association with aviation. In the course of this relationship, the Ente (canard, or duck) aircraft appeared. Its flying surfaces, as well as other components such as the undercarriage and fuel tank, were manufactured by Junkers in the Jco workshop. The fuselage was a steel frame roughly 10m (32ft 9¾in) long, at the rear of which was attached the corrugated metal-covered wings. For weight reasons, aluminium was selected as the working material. The powerplant was also situated at the rear, in this case a 70hp Argus motor driving a two-bladed pusher airscrew. As was customary with a canard layout, the tailplane was situated at the fuselage nose of what, in terms of today's standards, was a less than confidence-inspiring aircraft. The entire airframe was closely braced with wire for reasons of stability, and the daring aviator was seated in the rear half of the fuselage without any protection in a 'fresh-air' cockpit.

Reissner's 'wire cabinet' is said to have accomplished its maiden flight on 23rd May 1912. A number of photographs exist that show the Ente in various stages of construction. Unfortunately, it cannot be definitely established whether these are of the same aircraft or whether Reissner built a second example. On 27th January 1913 a fatal accident occurred when the pilot, Lucien Hild, who was neither wearing a protective helmet nor fastened by a safety-belt, was thrown out of the aircraft and killed when it descended in a rearward slide and crashed after failing to rise above some telephone lines. It is possible that later improvements were incorporated, which would account for the differences visible in the photographs.

Corrugated Sheeting: A Junkers Domain

As previously mentioned, during the First World War Junkers adopted the corrugated sheet method of construction. At first he used steel sheeting, then later duraluminium – a material that revolutionised aircraft manufacture. A closer look will now be taken at the composition and characteristics of this material.

In order to provide the relatively soft aluminium with greater structural strength, it was alloyed with various other metals, added in differing percentages. By way of example, the Fliegwerkstoff 3115 composition will be cited. The 'prescription' for this required the following percentage quantities of alloys:

- 3.7-4.7% Cu (copper)
- 0.6-1.0% Mg (magnesium)
- 0.2-0.4% Mn (manganese)
- 0.3-0.7% Si (silicon)
- 0.5% Fe (iron) and Ti (titanium)
- 0.1% Zn (zinc)
- Remainder, Al (aluminium)

The material attained machinability at a temperature of 650°C. For sheeting of up to 6mm thickness, a tensile strength of 42 to 46kg/mm² applied. With a specific weight of 2.8, this material was significantly lighter than the ferric materials hitherto used. The particular Werkstoff (raw material) mentioned was used for corrugations, strengthening bands, profiles, rods, tubing, and stamped as well as forged parts. The Fliegwerkstoff number system was introduced after 1934, whereby all such materials were identified by a corresponding first digit, that is 1 = steel, 2 = heavy metals, and 3 = light metals.

Duraluminium is traceable as an invention of the Dürener Metallwerke, based on the investigations of Ferdinand Wilm, who patented the idea in 1903, and since 1909 that firm had manufactured this light alloy composition suitable for aircraft construction. The details were contained in German Reichs Patent DRP 244,554 for hard aluminium, specifying 93% aluminium and 7% alloy materials, of which 3.5-4.5% was copper.

Duralumin (the registered name of the material), when worked in special machines into corrugated sheeting, offered the aircraft manufacturer a further advantage of structural strength, although by contrast the aerodynamist was anything but enthusiastic. Already during the First World War the visionary eye of Hugo Junkers had been drawn towards giant-sized civil aircraft. His ideas ranged towards the utopian proportions of aircraft accommodating up to 1,000 passengers, a vision that is only now being approached through today's technical advances. However, based more on reality was the Junkers Giant-Ente, soberly designated the J 1000, and the Junkerissime, which represented his intellectual outlook in the 1920s. Mention should also be made here of the large JG 1 aircraft, the construction of which had to be terminated in 1921 because of the limitations imposed by the Treaty of Versailles. The no less giant-sized R4, a three-engined monoplane like the J 1000 and the Junkerissime, remained only a project.

Naturally, because of their technical complexity projects, large aircraft such as the J 1000, with its 80m (262ft 5⅝in) wingspan, could only be realised in stages, represented by the F 13 civil aircraft type and its successors the G 24, the G 31 and the even more gigantic G 38, which more closely approached this ambitious aim. We shall now take a closer look at these intermediate stages.

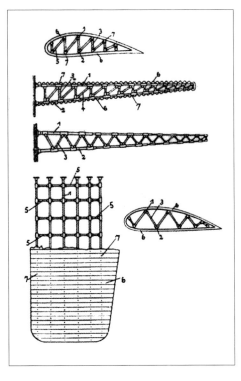

Junkers Patent drawing from DRP 337,522 illustrating a wing covered with corrugated sheet metal.

Technical Data for the Four Junkers 'Giant Aircraft'

Designation	R4	JG 1	Junkerissime	J 1000
Powerplant	Unknown	BMW IV	Junkers Diesel-oil motors	Junkers Diesel-oil turbines
Take-off power, hp	3 x unknown	4 x 250	4 x 700	4 x 1000
Wingspan	c38.00m (124' 8")	37.60m (123' 4¼")	62.80m (206' 0½")	80.00m (262' 5⅝")
Length	c24.00m (78' 8⅞")	18.00m (59' 0⅝")	31.20m (102' 4⅜")	24.00m (78' 8⅞")
Height	c5.50m (18' 0½")	4.70m (15' 5")	11.00m (36' 1⅛")	7.50m (24' 7¼")
Wing area, m^2 (ft^2)	c240 (2,583.28)	187.5 (2,018.18)	532 (5,726.26)	600 (6,458.19)
Equipped weight, kg (lb)	-	4,930 (10,869)	18,250 (40,234)	19,500 (42,990)
Flying weight, kg (lb)	-	9,000 (19,841)	30,000 (66,138)	36,000 (79,366)
Passengers and crew	24	9 + 2	56 + 7*	80 + 8†
Maximum speed	-	200km/h at 2,000m (124mph at 6,560ft)	200km/h (124mph) at sea-level	190km/h (118mph) at sea-level
Cruising speed	-	180km/h at 3,000m (112mph at 9,840ft)	180km/h (112mph) at sea-level	170km/h (106mph) at sea-level
Range, km (miles)	-	2,500 (1,553)	2,200 (1,367)	1,700 (1,056)
Service ceiling, m (ft)	-	6,000 (19,685)	-	3,600 (11,810)
Project year	-	1920	1920	1924
Remarks	-	Land version only	Land and floatplane versions*	Land version only. Canard layout

Note: In the book *Junkers und die Weltluftfahrt* (*Junkers and World Aviation*), published by Hauptmann F A Fisher von Poturzyn, Richard Pflaum Verlag, Munich, c1935, the following data on the above aircraft is to be found:

* Junkerissime (land version): Payload 13,200kg (29,100 lb), with a capacity for 60 passengers or freight at the speed and range quoted above. As a freight aircraft with 2,000kg (4,409 lb) of freight, maximum range was c4,000km (2,486 miles). The similar floatplane version, with similar twin fuselages and floats and of identical wingspan and wing area, had a length of 33.20m (108ft 11⅛in) and a horizontal height of 10.2m (33ft 5⅝in). The 60 passengers (or 40 in sleeper accommodation) and the freight areas were located in the wings and twin fuselages. With 60 passengers and baggage, the range was c1,350km (839 miles); the loaded weight is given as c40 tonnes (88,180 lb).

† For the J 1000 of 1924 with 100 passengers plus 10 crew, fuel was sufficient for 10 hours of full-power flight at 200km/h (124mph). Passenger space was divided into 12 cabins for 6 passengers and 14 cabins for 2 passengers. For night flights, the seats could be converted into sleeping berths. Other than rest rooms for the crew, it had two dining rooms for 18 persons each in both fuselages and additional rooms for wireless, mail, galley, toilets, and the like – Translator.

The Junkers F 13: The First All-metal Civil Aircraft

With the F13, Junkers developed the world's first all-metal civil transport aircraft, internal company research in the field of statics and aerodynamics being an important ingredient in its success. The principles of the Junkers method of design were also applied to the J 12, the plans for which were completed in January 1919 and pointed the way directly to the F 13. By today's standards, the design of this early airliner was completed in a very short time, with a mere 9,000 man-hours being needed for completion of the manufacturing drawings. As early as 25th June 1919 the prototype F 13 *Annelise* took to the air for the first time. The marketing problem was solved by Junkers in his own way. He participated, or appeared as co-founder, of various airline enterprises that were naturally also equipped with Junkers aircraft. Examples of these were the Trans-Europa Union and Junkers Luftverkehr, as well as foreign airlines such as the Columbian SCADTA and the Hungarian Aero Express.

The life of an F 13 in service with Luft Hansa from 1926 to 1939 can be exemplified by Werknummer 531 *Nachtigall* (Nightingale). Construction of this particular aircraft commenced on 10th February 1919 in Dessau, by the beginning of June it had reached its final assembly stage, and it accomplished its maiden flight during that same month. For ferrying purposes, it was accorded the provisional registration D-183, and following the completion of acceptance tests, it entered its air service role registered as D 1. From 13th April 1922 it became part of the fleet of Bayerische Luft Lloyd; Junkers provided this company with two F 13s in exchange for Junkers Luftverkehr being granted the regional concession. At the beginning of 1926 *Nachtigall* sported the colours of Luft Hansa. With effect from 20th March 1934, instead of the registration numbers there now followed an alphabet series of registrations whereby Werknummer 531 became D-OJOP. In April 1938 Luft Hansa transferred the aircraft to Hansa Flugdienst, which used the aircraft for round-trip flights. Its final destination was the Berlin Aircraft Collection at the Lehrter Bahnhof (railway terminal), where it became a victim of an Allied bombing raid during the Second World War. Following appropriate modifications, the machine belonged to the F 13 'bi' family, the letter 'b' signifying the version with an extended wing and the 'i' the BMW IV engine of 250hp. The F 13 designations ran to a total of some 60 variants, which for space reasons cannot be dealt with here.

Nachtigall was one of a total of 322 examples of the F 13. The last example was sold in 1932, and the 'Little One from Dessau' was at home all over the world. The highest number of registrations was in Germany, with 94 aircraft, followed by the USSR with 49. In third place stood the USA, with 26 Junkers Larsen JL 6s, which also flew for the US postal service. (John M Larsen, an American businessman of Danish ancestry, was the leading figure in visiting Dessau and bringing the F 13 into regular airline service in the USA. Junkers delivered 26 aircraft to the joint Junkers-Larsen Aircraft Corporation, founded in May 1920 – Translator.) The remainder were divided between 27 other countries, among them Poland with 16 and Italy with 12 aircraft.

There is no doubt that with the production of this aircraft the Junkers-Werke had raised itself significantly above the international standards of the time. Together with his ingenious Chief Designer, Dipl.-Ing. Otto Reuter, who died in 1922 at only 35 years of age, Hugo Junkers had paved the way and created the prerequisites for future aircraft types, leading via the G 24, G 31 and the W33/W34 series to the legendary 'Tante Ju' ('Aunty Ju', as the Ju 52 is affectionately known) and the G 38 – the Junkers 'Jumbo' of its day. With its appearance, the F 13 brought about a drastic change in air travel throughout the world.

The first all-metal transport aircraft in the history of civil aviation – the legendary Junkers F 13. (The first F 13, registered D 1, began commercial service in the summer of 1919 and was still operated by Luft Hansa 14 years later! – Translator.)

A particularly artistic impression of the larger Junkers G 24.

Technical Data for Junkers F 13 Variants

	F 13	F 13 de	F 13 keW
Powerplant	BMW IIIa	Junkers L5	Junkers L5
Take-off power, hp	1 x 185	1 x 310	1 x 310
Wingspan	14.82m (48' 7½")	17.75m (58' 2¾")	17.75m (58' 2¾")
Length	9.59m (31' 5½")	9.60m (31' 6")	10.10m (33' 1⅝")
Height	4.10m (13' 5⅜")	4.10m (13' 5⅜")	3.80m (12' 5⅝")
Wing area, m² (ft²)	34.50 (371.35)	43.00 (462.84)	44.00 (473.60)
Equipped weight, kg (lb)	1,975 (4,354)	1,225 (2,701)	1,390 (3,064)
Flying weight, kg (lb)	1,800 (3,968)	2,000 (4,409)	2,100 (4,630)
Max speed, km/h (mph)	170 (106)	192 (119)	182 (113)
Cruising speed	140 (87)	170 (106)	146 (91)
Range, km (miles)	1,200 (746)	980 (609)	875 (544)
Service ceiling, m (ft)	4,600 (15,090)	5,000 (16,400)	4,000 (13,120)
Passengers/crew	4/2	4/2	4/2

Three-Engined: The Junkers G 24

As conceived, the G 24 was to have been an enlarged F 13. Originally, designer Dipl.-Ing. Ernst Zindel had laid out the design as a single-engined aircraft, like the F 13. However, at that time there was no aero-engine of the required power available in Germany, neither could the numbers necessary for series production have been manufactured. Even if engines in the required quantities could have been delivered from abroad, lack of all-too-rare foreign exchange reserves would have made it impossible. Out of necessity, therefore, the G 24 was equipped with three engines of lesser power; a BMW IIIa was installed as the central motor, with two Mercedes D1 motors on the wings, all dating from the First World War. In this form and designated as the G 23, the first aircraft took off in absolute secrecy in Fürth. However, its morning flight on 19th September 1924 ended abruptly upon landing, although it was repaired in time for its second test flight on the 23rd.

In the years that followed, further G 23s were produced, and 12 were converted to G 24 standard by AB Flygindustri in Sweden, although their dimensions were less than those of the G 24 produced from 1925 onwards. Both models were manufactured in Dessau as well as in Sweden. A maximum of 70 G 24s (54 confirmed) were built, and during the course of production a host of variants appeared, summarised in brief as follows:

- G 23: Camouflage designation of the G 24 (previously called the J 24)
- G 24 ba: Version with three Junkers L2 motors. L2 deliveries followed in summer 1925
- G 24 b 1a: Float-equipped variant, powered by Junkers L2 motors.
- G 24 bi: Version with two Junkers L2 and one L5 motor.
- G 24 ce, de, fe: Three prototypes completed from the end of 1926. Alterations consisted of deeper wingroot centre sections, an enlarged vertical fin, and three L5 motors.
- G 24 c 1e, d 1e, f 1e: Water-based variants of the G 24 ce, de, fe
- G 24 ge: In this variant, the pilot was accommodated in a closed cockpit, had cabin heating and, later, radio equipment. Wheelbrakes were fitted, and powerplants were three L5 motors.
- G 24 g 1e: The corresponding floatplane version of the G 24 ge
- G 24 he: From this model onwards, wings of a deeper chord were installed, the wing profile having a raised trailing edge. Powerplants were three L5 motors that were now cowled.
- G 24 h 1e: Floatplane version equipped with larger floats and, compared to the G 24 he, an increased overall length of 16.70m (54ft 9½in)
- G 24 hu: As the G 24 but a one-off with 360hp BMW Va motors
- G 24 mai: Italian airline version powered by an Isotta-Fraschini Asso (Ace) in the fuselage nose and two Junkers L5 motors in the wings.
- G 24 nao: Bomber version powered by three 510hp Gnôme-Rhône Jupiter radials.

In addition to the above, there were the single-engined F 24 ko, kae, kai, kau and kay freight and civil variants, each fitted with differing powerplants. The Junkers K 30 was a military version based on the G 24. The K 30 a, b and c were produced from 1927 by AB Flygindustri. In 1928 Luft Hansa had the largest fleet of G 24s, with 28 examples; of these, nine were converted to F 24 ko standard and placed back in service during the years 1927-29.

The Legendary Ju 52

Even to its admirers, it is perhaps not well known that the Ju 52's early career was less than spectacular and, its future place and value in the rapidly developing air travel sector not yet appreciated, it began life as a single-engined freight aircraft. Its roots take us back to the year 1929, when the impulse for its development came from Junkers' idea of building up a principally air freight-oriented aircraft that would allow airlines to achieve a more solid financial footing beside the often not very economic passenger traffic. Ernst Zindel, to a certain extent the 'father' of this robust corrugated-sheet aircraft, laid out its foundations as early as 1926, based on the proven W 33, to which it was largely similar, with the exception of the powerplant. The design features of this Atlantic conqueror of 1928 certainly fulfilled the important characteristics of high robustness and reliability, but its spaciousness did not correspond to that of the new generation of freight-carrying aircraft. At this stage of its development it consisted purely of a freight aircraft having a 2,000kg (4,409 lb) payload, few frills, and, with a view to possibly lower operating costs, was only single-engined. However, thought was already being given to a follow-on passenger version, which had been taken into consideration in the course of design work.

As early as the summer of 1930, the first Ju 52 left the final assembly hall, and to the observer clearly displayed its lineage from the W 33. Although larger and more compact in appearance, it was similarly single-engined, and also featured the characteristic Junkers corrugated sheet skinning. The day of truth, when the theories had to be turned into reality, came on 11th September 1930, and Ernst Zindel was well satisfied with the results of the first flight of Werknummer 4001, bearing the registration D-1974. Unavoidable teething troubles, which beset almost every new design, had to be eliminated, but had only a temporary influence on further development. The most important of these was difficulties with control; these were dealt with by enlargement of the fin and the provision of an auxiliary balance weight for the elevator, which reduced the control forces required. Further test flights followed, culminating in the aircraft's DVL type-test in February 1931. Besides the civil sector, the military also began to display an even greater interest in the aircraft, while international familiarity with the Ju 52 began with a spectacular flight across the European continent.

In 1926 the network of routes flown was 20,408km (12,681 miles). Two years later this had expanded to 35,974km (22,354 miles). In 1926 Luft Hansa flew to 57 domestic destinations and 15 abroad, and within two years this had increased to 75 domestic and 24 abroad. In its first year the aircraft had carried 56,268 passengers, a figure that was almost double in 1928, at 111,115. In terms of air freight, encompassing both goods and mail, only 546 tonnes were registered in 1926, but two years later this had increased to 2,371 tonnes, a development that soon brought Luft Hansa to the limit of its capacity. Forecasts for the following year indicated further drastic growths in passenger and freight traffic that the G 24 and G 31 would not be capable of mastering, so these 'rosy' days could only be maintained with an aircraft

The Junkers Ju 52, the symbol of German transport aircraft of the day, was initially conceived as a single-engined aircraft.

The basic outlines of the Ju 52 are clearly recognisable in this W 34 (D-3159).

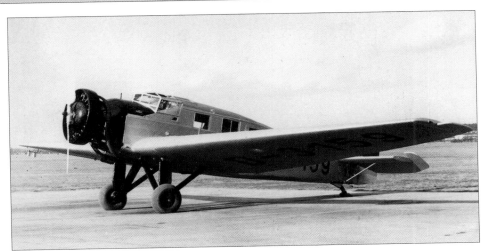

The next development step was the tri-motor Junkers G 31 de. Seen here is Werknummer 3002 (D-1310), christened *Hermann Köhl*.

designed to meet the needs of the period. At Junkers a solution to the problem duly appeared in the form of a three-engined version of the Ju 52. First flown in 1932, it typified the Junkers type of construction just as the F 13, the 'grandfather' of all modern airliners, had done more than a decade before in opening the door to a new era in air travel.

The first three-engined Ju 52 to join the Luft Hansa fleet was Ju 52/3mce Werknummer 4013, registered D-2201, in May 1932. This and subsequent machines, among them the Ju 52/3mfe, were powered by three 600hp Pratt & Whitney Hornet nine-cylinder radials. During the course of the aircraft's development, motive power was provided by a whole host of other engines. Their performance capabilities, as well as their robustness, were soon to be demonstrated by 'Tante Ju', when two occurrences in 1932 demonstrated the aircraft's behaviour in terms of the criteria that were absolutely necessary for success. On 28th July the pilot, Willi Polte, unsuspecting and in good spirits, was on his way back from the well-known Zürich Flying Meet. His route led him over the outskirts of Munich at Schleißheim, where the Deutsche Verkehrsfliegerschule (Transport Pilots School) was situated. One of the trainee pilots stationed there, flying a Udet Flamingo trainer aircraft, crossed the flight-path of Polte's Ju 52 and collided with the much larger Ju 52 with fatal results, the inattentiveness of the would-be pilot costing him his young life. The Ju 52, on the other hand, emerged with only minor bruises. Immediately after the collision, the Ju 52 deviated 90° to port and descended alarmingly fast towards the ground. With a torn-off port undercarriage, split-open flank, with one wing engine displaced from its anchoring and hanging like a drooping flower, Polte belly-landed the ruffled Ju 52 in a nearby rye field. After this involuntary fight between David and Goliath, the gaping wounds of the Junkers were repaired and the machine returned to service. Only four weeks later, Willi Polte, together with Erhard Milch – then the Luft Hansa Director – flew the same Ju 52 to an Alpine Flight Contest, which was won very easily. Neither Luft Hansa nor the manufacturer could have asked for a better commendation.

The charm of the 'Tante Ju' has already disappeared on this aircraft. Pictured here is a Ju 252 V1, the series production version of which was to replace the Ju 52/3m, and was further developed into the Ju 352. The Ju 52 nonetheless remained the standard transport up to the end of the Second World War.

The series-produced F 13 and G 31 seemed like dwarfs when compared with the J 1000 project.

The Junkers J 1000 'giant' project did not advance beyond the drawing-board and model stage.

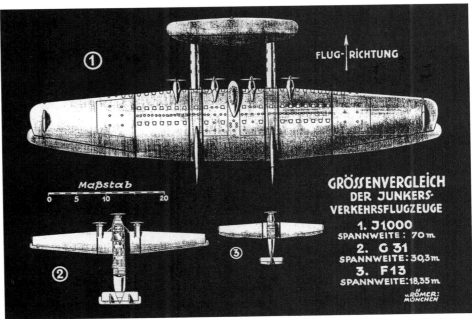

On the other side of the Atlantic, in the USA, a serious competitor for the proven 'Tante Ju' was soon emerging, for Donald Douglas was laying the foundation for a long series of airliners that are still successful today. On the basis of his first commercial aircraft, the one-off DC-1, Douglas produced the improved DC-2, for which Fokker possessed the sales rights in Europe. Compared to the rather heavy-looking Junkers, the design of this aircraft, which entered airline service in May 1934, was elegant and more aerodynamic in appearance. From the DC-2 was developed the optimised version, the DC-3, a 'best-seller' flown for the first time in December 1935 – clearly *the* airliner of the 1930s and 1940s. Both of these American aircraft were extensively used in European, especially for example by KLM, and thus became direct competitors to the rather conservatively-designed Ju 52.

In the Olympic year of 1936 Luft Hansa extended its fleet considerably, and no less than 85% of its aircraft consisted of the Ju 52/3m, whose reliability enabled the airline

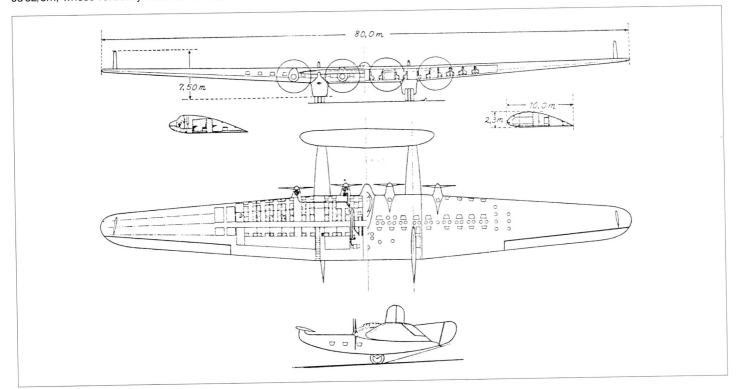

Top left: **A fictitious scene with the gigantic J 1000 as the centrepiece.**

Top right: **This 'giant' became a reality. With its 44m (144ft 4in) wingspan, it exceeded all previous standards. This view shows G 38 Werknummer 3302 (D-2500, later D-APIS) Generalfeldmarschall von Hindenburg.**

Above: **The two 'giants' of the early 1930s: the Dornier Do X (left) and the Junkers G 38 (D-2500 Generalfeldmarschall von Hindenburg).**

Below left: **The Junkers Ju 60, D-2400 Pfeil (Arrow). Junkers wanted this aircraft to compete with the fast Lockheed Orion, but to achieve this goal a departure from the traditional corrugated sheet skin was unavoidable.**

Below right: **A comparative view of the Lockheed Orion, which generated considerable uneasiness in the executive offices of European airlines and aircraft manufacturers. Swissair purchased two examples, and in reply to the superior Orion Heinkel brought out the sleek He 70.**

to maintain punctuality in its timetables. In airline service, a figure of 97% punctuality was achieved, and 90% of its winter schedules were maintained. Its safety record was also more than satisfactory: the accident rate per one million flying kilometres dropped from seven before the introduction of the Ju 52 to one-and-a-half, and from 1938 to less than one accident per million kilometres. But the clouds of war were soon to loom on the horizon, applying a brake to the rapid expansion of civil aviation. In 1940, although 80 Ju 52s of various models still flew for Lufthansa, their numbers were to dwindle rapidly in the years that followed, as they were largely assigned to military duties; in 1944 the fleet strength was a mere 24.

Peacetime usage of the Ju 52 was not limited to Germany, nor just to Lufthansa. Prior to September 1939 the Ju 52 flew under the flags of no fewer than 30 nations, and its international career, although not as widespread as that of the DC-3, nevertheless stretched from Denmark (Det Danske Luftfahrtselskab – DDL) to the southernmost tip of the African continent (South African Airways). In Europe, several 'Tante Ju' flew under the logo of the Belgian airline Sabena, as well as in Finland, Norway, Greece, Sweden (AB Aero Transport) and Italy (Ala Littoria). They also flew in Argentina, while in Bolivia a few Ju 52s flew for Lloyd Aereo Boliviano (LAB), and in Brazil several were in service with Syndicato Condor, together with two Focke-Wulf Fw 200 aircraft. With German participation, the Ju 52 was used by the Sino-German Eurasia airline in Mongolia as well as in the colours of the German-Russian Deruluft airline, which had a few in service.

In the years prior to the Second World War the Junkers-Werke order books were full, not only for civil aircraft but also significantly strengthened by military orders. Among the buyers was Switzerland, which ordered the aircraft for military use and, fortunately for our generation, has kept them in flying condition.

In conclusion, the Ju 52 doubtlessly represented a proverbial 'lucky shot' for the Junkers-Werke. Its operational spectrum ranged from extensive commercial use to the curious 'auxiliary' bomber during the early build-up of the Luftwaffe. It gained fame through spectacular flights in civil aviation, as well as in the transport role during operations that suffered heavy losses in the far hinterland of Russia and the singeing North African sun. Constantly encountered at the historical focal points of the time, the 'Tante Ju' undoubtedly earned its place in the family tree of German aviation, if not in the whole of aviation history.

Looking abroad, examples of corrugated-skin construction were also to be found in the USA, where the advantages of this type of construction were likewise recognised. Henry Ford produced a 'corrugated crate', the legendary Ford tri-motor, affectionately known as the 'Tin Goose'. Meanwhile, in Germany the path towards a pace-making civil transport was pursued by Junkers via the G 31, the G 38 and the Ju 86, the latter a modern flat-sheet-metal design. As a preliminary stage to the much larger Ju 90, the characteristics of the Ju 86 will now be described.

Aerodynamic 'Facelift': The Flat-sheet Construction Method of the Ju 86

The history of the Ju 86 stretches back to 1933, the year that the National Socialists (Nazis) assumed power. At that time Lufthansa was modernising its fleet, and required a fast twin-engined transport. The military also voiced such a requirement – a modern twin-engined bomber was called for to equip the still-secret Luftwaffe that was being brought into existence. Towards the end of 1933 a development contract was therefore awarded to the Junkers and Heinkel firms – all of which happened at a time when Hugo Junkers could no longer exercise any influence on the destiny of 'his' enterprise. Ernst Zindel was now responsible for design, and together with his team of engineers created an aircraft of flat sheet-metal skin construction. The Ju 86 was thus the first Junkers twin-engined aircraft to dispense with the corrugated sheet-metal type of construction.

The principal purchaser for the civil version was undoubtedly Lufthansa, which had already declared its need for this category of aircraft at the beginning of 1933. The RLM, on the other hand, only accepted it with the stipulation that aircraft delivered to Lufthansa should be capable of conversion at any time into a military configuration by means of Rüstsätze (field equipment sets) to suit its corresponding operational use. During the initial stage of the Ju 86 production programme, every second machine was to be turned out as a civil aircraft. Eighteen months after the date of the contract, the first prototype stood ready to make its maiden flight on 4th November 1934. Since the intended 600hp Jumo 205 diesel engines were not yet available, they had to be unwillingly replaced by two Siemens SAM 22 radials, each of 550hp take-off power. Series manufacture of the Jumo 205 did not commence until April 1935, by which time the Ju 86 had long been undergoing flight-testing. During these tests it displayed serious faults, eliminated by design alterations in the form of a modified mass-balance for the rudder, which resulted in a positive effect on control behaviour, and the strengthening of the structure in the region of the fuselage.

In Rechlin, there were not inconsiderable problems with the Ju 86 V1, which concerned a tendency to dive and spin. Rechlin pilot Flugbaumeister Hans Sander reported that some mechanics refused to accompany them on test flights, as the Ju 86 appeared to them to be too risky. The reason for this dangerous behaviour during flight and also on landing, according to an analysis by Ernst Zindel, was traceable to its sharply tapered wing planform. The second (civil version) prototype, the V2, was the first Ju 86 to be equipped with the Jumo 205 diesel engines, followed in the long series of prototypes by the Ju 86 V3, a military prototype. As with the V1, this was equipped with appropriate weapon stations. Powered by two Pratt & Whitney Hornet radials, the V3 accomplished its first flight on 16th June 1936, followed by the V4, completed as a civil variant; this airframe was delivered to Lufthansa but suffered a fair amount of damage in a crash landing in July 1937. In December 1935 the V5 left the final assembly line in Dessau and was the first of the aircraft taken out of the 0-series. The most important design change compared to its predecessors was the newly configured wing with significantly improved aerodynamic characteristics. This served as the model for the military Ju 86A-I version, while the Ju 86 V6, V7 and V8 prototypes also served a military purpose.

The Ju 86 V9 was handed over to the Hansa Luftbild GmbH air-photography company, an organisation serving as a camouflage for the special-purpose military Fliegerstaffel. The V10 and V11 served as prototypes for the Ju 86A-0 series, while the V12, likewise a military prototype, was powered by BMW 132 radials in place of the Jumo 205 engines; various sources also mention use of the Pratt & Whitney Hornet as the powerplant. The V14 and V15 were flown with Jumo 207 engines, whereas the V16, equipped with the BMW 132, served as the prototype for the Ju 86G, regarded as the most advanced variant. The last of the prototypes was the V24, equipped with the BMW 132, which entered service with Lufthansa. Over the coming years, this airline, established in 1926, had no fewer than 14 of these aircraft of differing models.

We now turn to the technicalities of the Ju 86 – or to be more exact, the Ju 86B. The fuselage, of semi-monocoque all-metal dural construction, had a length of 17.60m (57ft 8⅞in); this was increased, for example on the Ju 86K, to 17.87m (58ft 7½in), while in the case of the Ju 86P and R the length was reduced to 16.45m (53ft 11⅝in). For the civil version, the nose was covered with sheet metal. The two-crew cockpit section located behind the nose had auxiliary controls in front of the right-hand seat. The fuselage featured an oval cross-section and besides the crew of two could accommodate ten passengers; $3.50m^3$ ($123.6ft^3$) of space was available for the latter's luggage.

The empennage, likewise of all-metal construction, completed the fuselage structure at the rear. Consisting of twin endplate fins and rudders, the tailplane had a span of 6.80m (22ft 3¾in) and an area of $9.96m^2$ ($107.21ft^2$). The whole unit was mounted atop the fuselage structure and supported by an external strut on

either side. The endplate vertical surfaces had a total area of 6.34m² (68.24ft²), but unlike the rest of the metal-covered structure, both rudders and elevator were covered with fabric. To reduce the control forces, the rudders had external weight as well as aerodynamic balances. The Ju 86C differed in having a lengthened tailcone and modified radiator cowlings.

The wing was of all-metal monocoque construction. On the Ju 86B, the wingspan was 22.50m (73ft 9⅞in) and the wing area 82.00m² (882.62ft²). On the Ju 86P and R high-altitude reconnaissance versions, span and area were both greatly increased: for the Ju 86P, the figures were 25.60m (83ft 11⅞in) and 92.00m² (990.26ft²), while on the Ju 86R the corresponding measurements were 32.00m (104ft 11⅞in) and 97.50m² (1,049.5ft²) respectively. The wings contained several fuel tanks. On the Ju 86B, the total fuel capacity was 1,500 litres, together with 140 litres of lubricant. As with the earlier G 31, this aircraft also featured the so-called Junkers 'double wing', where the entire wing trailing edge controls – the combined

ailerons and flaps – were detached from the main wing structure. The total area of these surfaces was divided into 4.52m² (48.65ft²) for the ailerons and 8.16m² (87.83ft²) for the flaps. The wing was covered with flat dural sheeting throughout.

In the course of production, several types of powerplants were installed in the Ju 86. These ranged from German engines to those of British, French, and American origin. The present description is, however, limited to the two most important types of the former: the BMW 132 and the Jumo 205. The latter was a robust so-called Schwerölmotor (heavy-oil diesel-type engine), which was intended for installation right from the very beginning, but was initially available in only very limited numbers. Although this powerplant passed its type-test in the spring of 1933, the first series examples could not be delivered before 1935. In civilian use, hardly any problems were experienced with the Jumo 205, where the time between overhauls stood at 250 hours. By contrast, the military had a less positive opinion of it, based

on very different criteria: continually changing flying altitudes, permanent rpm changes and, not least, operation at high altitudes taxed the engines considerably. Undoubtedly, under these conditions a greater performance spectrum was required of the engines than in Lufthansa's network over the Atlantic, where long stretches could be flown at low altitudes and constant rpm.

The Jumo 205 was termed an opposed-piston engine, its six twin-piston cylinders located vertically above and below the crankshafts. Power was transmitted to the propellers via a radially-arranged (0.63) reduction gearing. Total capacity of the cylinders was 16.6 litres, and with the Jumo 205A/B and Jumo 205C the take-off power was 600hp at 2,200rpm. On the Jumo 205D of 1940, take-off power rose to 880hp at 2,800rpm. Power for the Ju 86B was provided by two Jumo 205C motors. From an international point of view, the Jumo 205 was the sole diesel aero-engine possessing high operating safety, and licence manufacturing rights for the 205D were secured by Napier in England and Lilloise in France.

The radial engine developed by BMW employed a completely different technology, and the history of this motor, as well as its technical details, are described in a later section of this book. The first examples of the BMW 132 became available to airframe manufacturers in 1933, and in the course of Ju 86 production, by way of examples, the following variants of this unit were installed:

- Ju 86E, G and H: BMW 132F/N
- Ju 86K-3: BMW 132Da
- Ju 86Z-2: BMW 132Dc and H/1

The Ju 86 was the first twin-engined Junkers airliner to feature the more progressive flat-sheet method of skinning. The photo is of a Ju 86 in the colours of Swiss Air Lines.

The development of passenger capacity of various Junkers aircraft designs.

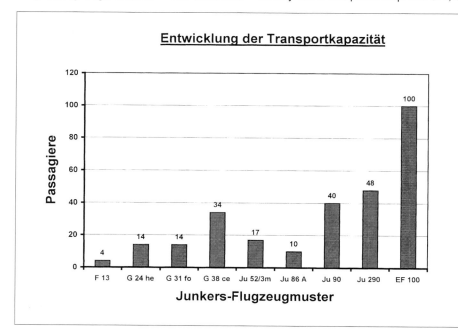

Entwicklung der Transportkapazität

Passagiere / Junkers-Flugzeugmuster

Junkers-Flugzeugmuster	Passagiere
F 13	4
G 24 he	14
G 31 fo	14
G 38 ce	34
Ju 52/3m	17
Ju 86 A	10
Ju 90	40
Ju 290	48
EF 100	100

The total weight of the airframe components and installations in the Ju 86B was 5,790kg (12,765 lb) and take-off weight was close to 8,000kg (17,637 lb). Maximum speed was 310km/h (193mph) at sea-level, with a cruising speed of 280km/h at 1km (174mph at 3,280ft). Lufthansa had a total of 14 examples of the Ju 86B-1, C-1 and Z-2 aircraft. The first six machines were on its inventory in 1936, and while serving on its commercial routes one Ju 86 was lost. In 1940 12 aircraft were transferred to the RLM for military usage, the last remaining aircraft following in 1941.

The Ju 86 did not only fly under the German flag, as the Junkers-Werke was also successful in awaking interest in it abroad, and obtaining the corresponding permission for its export. Such was the case with neighbouring Switzerland. Further aircraft exported were the Ju 86K-1 and K-4 military variants, sold to Sweden. Hungary purchased several of the Ju 86K-2 variant, while Portugal purchased the Ju 86K-7, and the robust Ju 86 was even to be seen in distant Chile. These export variants were designated as the K-6; the 'K' sub-type indicated that these were a military version of the Ju 86, whereas civil-use export versions bore the letter 'Z', in designations from Ju 86Z-1 to Z-7. The Ju 86Z-1 corresponded to the Ju 86C-1 series and was powered by the Jumo 205. A further Ju 86Z-1 order was received by the Chilean airline LAN (Linea Aerea National), which in 1938 ordered four examples powered by the Pratt & Whitney Hornet.

Additionally, in 1938 the Junkers-Werke received an order from the Manchurian Gov-

Technical Data for the Ju 86

Model	Ju 86A	Ju 86B	Ju 86Z
Powerplant	Jumo 205C	Jumo 205C	BMW 132Dc
Take-off power, hp	600	600	845
Take-off speed, rpm	2,200	2,200	1,690
Wingspan	22.50m (73' 9⅞")	22.50m (73' 9⅞")	22.50m (73' 9⅞")
Length	17.44m (57ft 2⅝")	17.60m (57ft 9")	17.60m (57ft 9")
Height	4.08m (13ft 4⅝")	4.70m (15ft 5")	4.70m (15ft 5")
Wing area, m² (ft²)	82.00 (882.62)	82.00 (882.62)	82.00 (882.62)
Equipped weight, kg (lb)	5,520 (12,169)	5,790 (12,765)	5,900 (13,007)
Take-off weight, kg (lb)	8,000 (17,637)	7,850 (17,306)	8,200 (18,078)
Wing loading, kg/m² (lb/ft²)	97.56 (19.98)	95.73 (19.61)	100 (20.48)
Max speed, km/h (mph)	310 (193)	310 (193)	375 (233)
Cruising speed, km/h (mph)	285 (177)	280 (174)	340 (211)
Range, normal, km (miles)	1,200 (746)	1,500 (932)	1,000 (621)
Range, max, km (miles)	-	2,000 (1,242)	1,500 (932)
Service ceiling, m (ft)	6,100 (20,015)	5,900 (19,360)	6,900 (22,640)
Passengers/crew	10/4	10/2-3	10/2-3

ernment for 20 examples of the civilian Ju 86, and the aircraft was even to be found at the southern tip of the African continent. South African Airways purchased 17 examples of the Ju 86Z-5, powered by the Rolls-Royce Kestrel and the Pratt & Whitney Hornet. The Ju 86Z-7 was a special variant tailored for postal flights, powered by the Hornet, and one aircraft of this model was ordered by Sweden.

Besides its routine use on airline routes or in rougher conditions of military service, the Ju 86 attained a whole host of impressive individual achievements. Compared to the enormous number of 8,000 examples of the Heinkel He 111, a mere 840 examples of the Ju 86 were

built for civil and military purposes; in the latter sphere the He 111 was far superior to the Ju 86. In the category of military aircraft, Junkers was first able to secure the proverbial 'big throw' with the Ju 88, which, like the He 111, served on all fronts as a standard bomber and night-fighter. With the availability of more modern types of aircraft, the Ju 86 'stop-gap' was soon replaced on the front line of the Luftwaffe's formations.

The Ju 86 was built in Germany both as a civil aircraft and as a bomber and reconnaissance aircraft. Nearest the camera is Lufthansa's Ju 86B-1 (D-AQER) *Inselsberg*, and beyond it Ju 86C-1 (D-AKOI) *Kaiserstuhl*.

Chapter Two

Warbird

The Strategic Bomber

The Path to the Ju 89

As in the days of the First World War, when, unusually at that time, the giant Gotha, VGO or Staaken large bombers took the war to the enemy, the new still-secret Luftwaffe was also to be equipped with this same capability in the Second. When considering developments in, for example, Great Britain or the USA, it becomes obvious that the trend was unequivocally in the direction of the strategic bomber. But even here there were numerous problems that had first to be overcome, problems that were not only of a technical nature. Following long controversy amongst the leadership, the necessity for these aircraft was also realised in the new Luftwaffe. The direction to be followed had been altered, but for only a short period, and the result was that two four-engined bombers began to take shape in the form of the Junkers Ju 89 and its competitor, the Dornier Do 19. In accordance with the controversial doctrine propounded by the Italian General Giulio Douhet, and the lesser-known French Navy Chief Engineer Camille Rougeron, long-range bombers capable of penetrating deep into the heart of enemy territory and destroying industries and vital infrastructures were now to make their appearance. As early as 1926, Major Helmuth Wilberg, an officer in the Truppenamt (Armed Forces Office), had held this viewpoint, even before Oberst Walter Wever, who was likewise a strong supporter of the long-range bomber and who had at least made a beginning by turning the concept into a reality. This 'beginning' explains the curricula vitae of the two aircraft types that now appeared.

The Ju 89 V1 and V2 Prototypes

The initial steps that led to the Ju 89 can be traced back to mid-1933, and took on a more tangible form in October 1933 when Junkers was asked to submit an appropriate design proposal. During the ensuing months a firm order was issued with a completion target for the first prototype of October 1936. According to further plans, the Ju 89 V1 was to commence flight trials at Rechlin in February 1937. Commencement of development of the Do 19 can also be traced back to mid-1933. Both aircraft had initially been accorded the highest priority,

but after a relatively short time this priority rating was drastically altered. In May 1934 the large bombers' priority preceded even that of the heavy dive-bomber, the medium bomber, and that of the Zerstörer (twin-engined heavy fighter) and high-altitude reconnaissance aircraft. The ready-to-fly dates decided upon were:

- Ju 89 V1: October 1937
- Ju 89 V2: December 1937
- Ju 89 pre-production aircraft: December 1937 on

In the meantime, the Ju 89 V1 prototype had been completed and had accomplished its maiden flight on 11th April 1937, followed by the first flight of the Ju 89 V2 on 12th August. In June 1938 the Ju 89 V2 set two payload world records: with a 5,000kg (11,023 lb) payload it reached an altitude of 9,312m (30,551ft), and with a 10,000kg (22,046 lb) payload it reached 7,242m (23,760ft). In order to increase the sales possibilities of the Ju 90, these impressive figures were ascribed to the latter aircraft. Originally, the Ju 89 V3 and nine pre-production machines were to have followed, but the RLM had now undergone a drastic change of perception to the detriment of the strategic bomber, so that the third prototype of the Ju 89 was completed as the Ju 90.

In accordance with modern methods of construction, the Ju 89 was of semi-monocoque construction covered with smooth all-metal skinning. The fuselage, of rectangular cross-section, had a length of 26.30m (86ft 3½in), and featured a completely glazed nose with bracing separating the individual panels. Above this was the so-called 'glasshouse' that accommodated a crew of two seated in tandem. The nose of the Ju 89 V1 was fitted with a projecting mast for securing the measuring instruments, the fuselage rear terminating in large tail surfaces with twin endplate fins and rudders. In its initial state, the horn balances that reduced rudder forces were not fitted. In addition, a provisional tail armament position stemming from a Ju 86 A-Stand was installed.

The wing of the Ju 89 was of no lesser proportions. Trapezoidal in its geometry and of deep chord, it had an impressive span of 35m (114ft 10in) and an area of 184m² (1,980.5ft²). The low-positioned wing was made up of four sections and supported the four Daimler-Benz DB 600C powerplants, each of 910hp driving

three-bladed Junkers-Hamilton variable-pitch airscrews, later replaced by VDM airscrews. It had originally been planned to equip the aircraft with Jumo 211 engines, but these were still undergoing testing at the time. For the DB 600C motors, a total of 3,000kg (6,614 lb) of fuel and 300kg (661 lb) of lubricant was available, the tanks being incorporated in the wings.

Added to the equipped weight of 16,000kg (35,274 lb) was 3,300kg (7,275 lb) of fuel and oil, a payload of 1,000kg (2,205 lb) and 500kg (1,102 lb) for the crew, giving an impressive total weight of 20,800kg (45,856 lb). The corresponding load was supported on an undercarriage similar to that of the Ju 90. This consisted of a so-called forked undercarriage used in combination with a tailwheel. These rolling components had hydraulically operated twin wheels fitted with brakes, and measured 1450 x 500mm (57.1 x 19.7in), the tailwheel measuring 950 x 350mm (37.4 x 13.8in).

As previously mentioned, besides the V1 and V2 there was to have been a third prototype, but because of revised guidelines issued in the interim that had pushed the strategic bomber aside, the V3 now appeared as the Ju 90. The initial steps to complete the V3, not as a bomber, were already documented in 1935. Proof of this is contained in the Aircraft Development Programme of the RLM Technisches Amt (Technical office), which, in November 1935 and January 1936, termed the V3 as a 'Lufthansa civil variant'.

The Ju 89 V3, or rather those of its components that that were actually used in the manufacture of the Ju 90 V1, would certainly never have been capable of being made ready to fly in such a short period of time. As cited above, the Ju 89 V2 had flown for the first time on 12th August 1937, the Ju 90 V1 following on 28th August. It is therefore obvious that construction of the V3 had already begun, tailored to a Lufthansa configuration, that is with a high-capacity fuselage. Thus only the wings and undercarriage from the V3 would have been usable, its completely new purpose requiring the expansive fuselage of a civil aircraft. Because of the necessarily extensive preparatory work involved, this could not have been realised in the space of only a few months. Hence, based on the reasons mentioned above, it can be proved that manufacture of the V3 had already begun as a civil aircraft. By the

Side view of the Ju 89 V1, which took off on its maiden flight on 11th April 1937.

Three-quarter rear view of the Ju 89 V1. The tail gun position consisted of a ball turret that formed the A-Stand on the Ju 86.

The Ju 89 V1 (D-AFIT) pictured in 1937, now fitted with dorsal mass-balances on each of the endplate rudders.

In this frontal view, the instrument probe beneath the nose of the Ju 89 V1 served to measure airspeed precisely.

Aircraft Development Programme of April 1937 the Ju 89 V3 was no longer being taken into account.

What were the circumstances that brought about the downfall of the Ju 89 and Do 19 large bomber projects? Among the most significant facts was a directive from General Walter Wever shortly before his death, in which new guidelines were contained that indicated a path towards the He 177 and other projects whose performance requirements had been raised to conform with progressive standards. It was clear to Wever that the Ju 89 and its competitor, the Do 19, were to be regarded merely as experimental types. The lack of suitable power-plants was also responsible. As indicated, the two in-line engines as well as the DB 601 had not been sufficiently tested at this time, so faced with an emergency situation, the choice fell on the DB 600. Yet despite all hindrances, the actual flight-cleared date was considerably in advance of that stipulated by the purchaser.

In the previous year a further important factor had been added when Ernst Udet, an audacious pilot of the time and anything but an armchair administrator, took over the reins from Oberst Wilhelm Wimmer, Chief of the RLM Technisches Amt. Udet was the staunch champion of the dive-bomber, and it was not long before the legendary 'Stukas' employed in Spain were to demonstrate before the eyes of the world the possibilities of this weapon. The instrument for the Blitzkrieg (lightning war) had been born. Attention then turned to bomb-carrying aircraft of smaller dimensions, and there were several reasons why the large bomber was now being regarded as the proverbial 'neglected child'. For one thing, tactics were now geared to the dive- and medium bomber, and alterations to this would naturally require drastic modifications in the planned numbers in the aircraft inventory. The decision in favour of aircraft of smaller dimensions took into account limited production capacities, and the far from inexhaustible availability of raw materials and fuel. Indeed, at an advanced stage in the Second World War the latter, together with other factors, was to 'break the back' of the Luftwaffe. In addition to insufficient manufacturing capac-

ity for the large bomber, there was also a lack of qualified personnel to build the aircraft. In view of this situation, the other side of the Atlantic was looked upon with jealous eyes, where, in the USA, production was soon to take on gigantic proportions.

As a result of these certainly indisputable factors, the new philosophy gave an immense lift to the dive- and medium bomber. Aircraft in this category required far less precious duraluminium and other raw materials that were not available in unlimited quantities. The path was thus paved for the Ju 87, Ju 88, He 111 and Do 17, all of which certainly fitted better into the later successful Blitzkrieg concept that within a very short time would lead to the defeat of Poland in 1939.

Some two-and-a-half years earlier, in April 1937, the Large Bomber Programme was therefore officially terminated, and certainly took place at Hermann Göring's bidding through Wever's successor, General Albert Kesselring. During the build-up phase of the Luftwaffe, this decision was undoubtedly correct. However, it was ultimately proved wrong when the call came to conduct an effective bomber offensive against the British Isles. Due to insufficient range, low bombloads and insufficient fighter protection, poor results were obtained that resulted not only in a lost 'Battle of Britain', but also distinct disadvantages in other operations. Something similar happened when the Luftwaffe was called upon but failed to destroy Soviet industry beyond the Urals, as such problems were already becoming evident in earlier years.

The proverbial 'sovereign remedy' was now to be the He 177. But this aircraft also had its own design-oriented problems, the principal of which lay in the powerplants, suffering accordingly in operational use. The engine problem here was the result of a long pause in development after the First World War, but this was another 'unending story' that ran like the oft-cited 'red thread' through the history of the Luftwaffe. The coupled engine was certainly not developed as a result of ultimate wisdom. The hope lay in the Jumo 222, but this had been literally 'developed to death'. To conclude

this topic, the following point should be made: even if the German four-engined bomber (leaving aside the He 177) could have been produced in large numbers, to have been able to accomplish its duties effectively it would have required an extensively infrastructure. But where did this exist – at least for front-line formations that would have been equipped with comparable large four-engined aircraft? Airfields within the Reich and in the occupied territories were year after year more and more exposed to the continually growing strength of Allied air fleets. The Allies, particularly the Americans, were able through enormous industrial efforts to produce a giant armada of Boeing B-17 Flying Fortresses, since the necessary resources were available. The Allies thus held the trumps, and it was only a matter of time before German cities, industries and communications networks would be decimated. The Luftwaffe's capabilities, when compared with this potential, have to be regarded as rather poor. Nevertheless, it was able, at least for a limited period and at the cost of a horrendous loss of Dornier, Heinkel, and Junkers bombers, to cause considerable damage, for example in England. German losses weighed far more heavily than on the Allied side, as the aircrews and machines were more difficult to replace.

The success of the Allied bomber offensive was therefore due to the following important criteria:

- Considerably intact airfields
- Adequate replacement of aircrews, aircraft, spare parts and fuel
- Effective fighter protection

All these were factors that during the continuation of the war applied less and less to the Luftwaffe and which inevitably had to lead to its downfall.

But to return now to the pre-war era, and to the subject of the Ju 89 and its rivals, as already mentioned a mere three examples of the Ju 89 were actually built. How did their future destiny progress?

Ju 89 V1
Werknummer 4911 (D-AFIT)

This prototype completed its last works flight on 2nd September 1938 and shortly afterwards was delivered to the Luftwaffe. Both the Ju 89 V1 and the Do 19 were placed under Flugkommando (Flight Detachment) Berlin, a training organisation for Luftwaffe personnel that in peacetime was subordinated to Lufthansa. In the event of mobilisation, this unit, together with Lufthansa aircraft, was to form Transportgeschwader 172. The Ju 89 V1 was attached to Flugkommando Berlin until the end of September 1938, thereafter disappearing from view, and reportedly being scrapped in May 1939.

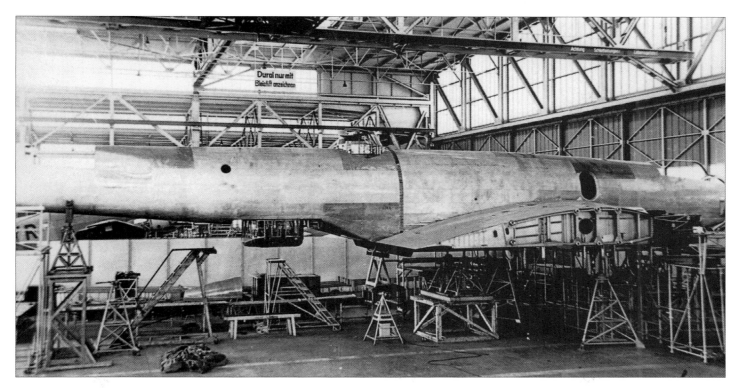

Top: **The fuselage of the Ju 89 V2. (The notice in the background above it says 'Dural to be inscribed only in pencil' – Translator.)**

Above left: **Due to the slim fuselage, the two crew seats were positioned in tandem.**

Above right: **Details of the ventral C-Stand on the Ju 89 V2.**

Right: **This view shows the enormous difference in size between the various categories of bombers. Pictured here is the Ju 89 V2 and, behind it, the Ju 88 V1.**

Photograph on the opposite page:

The Ju 89 V1 preparing for take-off.

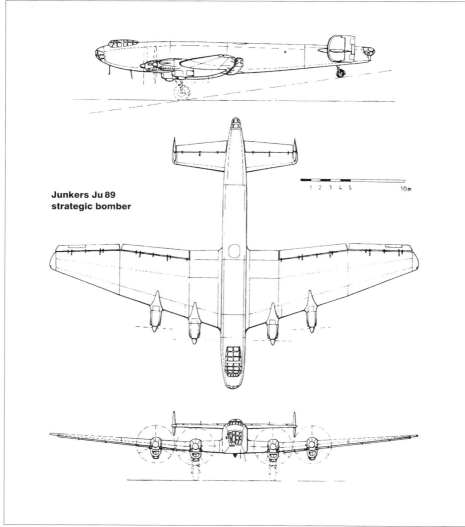

**Junkers Ju 89
strategic bomber**

1 2 3 4 5   10 m

The Ju 89 doubtless possessed an enormous development potential.

Ju 89 V2
Werknummer 4912 (D-ALAT)

This prototype took off on its last works flight on 29th September 1938, being subsequently transferred to Flugkommando Berlin, where it was camouflaged in RLM colours 70/71/65. Subsequently no definite traces of it have been unearthed. What is known is that a Ju 89 (Werknummer unknown) was, for a short period at least, parked in the hangar on Löwenthal airfield (Dornier, Friedrichshafen). The other example most probably served as a bombing target on a training ground near Berlin, but even in this case its identity cannot be established. After a short flying life, the Ju 89 V2 fell into the hands of a scrap dealer in November 1938.

Ju 89 V3

The fate of this prototype is definitely on record. Originally planned as a bomber, it was 'converted' at an early date and completed as the Ju 90 V1 prototype, accomplishing its maiden flight on 28th August 1937. The further history of this particular aircraft forms a special section of this narrative, so first its competitor from the house of Dornier will be dealt with. The Dornier-Werke GmbH also possessed considerable experience in the realm of large aircraft manufacture, exemplified by the giant Do X, which made its appearance in many parts of the world.

The Competitor: Dornier Do 19

The origin of this equally luckless design also dates back to 1933. Its initial outlines took shape in July of that year, and on 24th February 1934 Dornier received a contract for construction of a full-scale mock-up. Particular value was placed on the aircraft's effective defence capability, since its dimensions undoubtedly presented a large target area. Naturally, as with aircraft of this size, its manoeuvrability was not of the best. Exactly one year to the day after the construction contract for the mock-up, Dornier received an order for the manufacture of the Do 19 V1 and V2. That this would not eventually progress beyond the completion of a sole prototype could not be known to anyone – at least not at the Dornier firm.

The Do 19 V1 was powered by the Siemens (Bramo) SAM 322 engines, while the Do 19 V2 was intended to have the BMW 132F. The BMW 133 or 135 were also considered, but their development was discontinued. For the planned third prototype, the engines used by the V2 were intended for installation. Following completion, the three aircraft, Werknummern 701, 702 and 703, were to have been thoroughly tested by the Reichsverband der Deutschen Luftfahrtindustrie (Reich Association of the German Aviation Industry) in Rechlin. However, only the Do 19 V1 (D-AGAI) was completed, and took to the air for the first time on 28th October 1936. Subsequently test flights amounting to a total of more than 32 hours were conducted over 83 days. In October 1938 the prototype stood ready for use by Transportgeschwader 172, and is confirmed as having been stationed there until May 1939. At this time, however, the dice had long since been thrown and termination of the entire project had been already decided by the Luftwaffe. Together with the two Ju 89s, this giant bird would soon be degraded to the status of scrap metal.

As early as July 1936 the zero or pre-series aircraft had already been cancelled, and in August Dornier received the instruction to terminate the project. Despite forceful intervention on Dornier's part, which did not succeed in changing anything, he terminated all further work on the aircraft in October. Dornier likewise failed to rescue the Do 19 in the form of a passenger or freight-carrying aircraft, which he wanted to present to the RLM under the project designations P 30-12 and P 30-13. In the first-named configuration, it would accommodate 30 passengers, and in the second 22. In this connection it should be remarked that even before Dornier had protested, the RLM as well as Lufthansa had firmly rejected the development of a civil Do 19. Lufthansa Director Karl August von Gablenz argued that the airline already had the large land-based Fw 200 and the Ju 90 aircraft under development. As

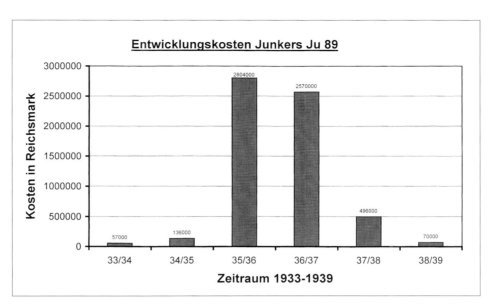

Entwicklungskosten Junkers Ju 89

Kosten in Reichsmark

Zeitraum	Kosten
33/34	57000
34/35	136000
35/36	2804000
36/37	2570000
37/38	496000
38/39	70000

Zeitraum 1933-1939

Top: **Costs in Reichsmarks during the period 1937-39 include those for the Ju 89 V3 that was completed as the Ju 90 V1.**

Centre: **The rival to the Ju 89 was the Dornier Do 19, which first flew on 26th October 1936.**

Bottom: **For a while, a glazed ventral pannier was installed beneath the forward fuselage.**

Above: **Frontal view of the Do 19 V1. Like the Ju 89, its wingspan was exactly 35 metres.**

Left: **The sole Do 19 V1, registered D-AGAI, had grey lettering on the fuselage sides.**

Bottom: **Neither the Do 19 nor the Ju 89 succeeded in entering series manufacture. Years later, British and American bombers displayed the capabilities of this type of aircraft in a dramatic way.**

Photographs on the opposite page:

Left: **The nine-cylinder Bramo 322 air-cooled radial.**

Right: **A close-up of the four Bramo 322J-2 motors that powered the Do 19 V1.**

Technical Data Comparisons Between the Ju 89, Do 19 and Comparable American Aircraft

Manufacturer / Aircraft	Junkers Ju 89	Dornier Do 19	Martin XB-16	Boeing XB-17	Douglas XB-19
Powerplant	Daimler-Benz	Bramo	Allison	Pratt & Whitney	Wright
Model	DB 600C	322J-2	V-1710	Hornet	R-3350
Take-off power, hp	4 x 910	4 x 715	4 x 1000	4 x 750	4 x 2000
Fuel capacity	3,000kg	3,500 litres	16,040 litres	6,440 litres	38,178 litres
Wingspan	35.00m (114' 10")	35.00m (114' 10")	42.67m (140' 0")	31.63m (103' 9")	64.62m (212' 0")
Length	26.30m (86' 3.4")	25.45m (83' 6")	25.60m (84' 0")	20.96m (68' 9")	40.34m (132' 4")
Height	6.50m (21' 3.9")	5.77m (18' 11")	5.97m (19' 7")	4.57m (15' 0")	12.80m (42' 0")
Wing area, m² (ft²)	184.00 (1,980.5)	162.00 (1,743.7)	241.55 (2,600)	131.92 (1,420)	398.09 (4,285)
Equipped weight, kg (lb)	16,000 (35,274)	11.940 (26,323)	14,495 (31,956)	9,823 (21,656)	39,000 (85,980)
Take-off weight, kg (lb) normal	20,800 (45,856)	18,500 (40,785)	-	14,711 (32,432)	63,503 (140,000)
maximum	27,800 (61,288)	-	29,484 (65,000)	17.482 (38,540)	73,260 (161,510)
Max speed, km/h (mph)	410 (255)	314 (195)	381 (237)	380 (236)	360 (224)
Cruising speed, km/h (mph)	310 (193)	270 (168)	193 (120)	225 (140)	217 (135)
Range, normal, km (miles)	1,300 (808)	1,450 (901)	8,111 (5,040)	3,283 (2,040)	8,369 (5,200)
Range, max, km (miles)	2,980 (1,852)	-	9,978 (6,200)	4,990 (3,100)	12,408 (7,710)
Service ceiling, m (ft)	7,000 (22,965)	5,600 (18,375)	6,858 (22,500)	7,504 (24,620)	7,010 (23,000)
Bombload, kg (lb)	1,600 (3,527)	2,945 (6,493)	5,525 (12,180)	2,177 (4,800)	16,828 (7,100)
Armament (intended)	2 x MG FF	4-5 MG 15	-	5 x 7.62mm MG	1 x 37mm MK
	2 x MG 15	-	-	-	5 x 12.7mm MG
	-	-	-	-	6 x 7.62mm MG
Crew	5	7	10	8	16-18
First flight date	11.04.1937	26.10.1936	Project. (Development begun 1934, Model 145A)	28.07.1935	27.06.1941 (Development begun 1935)
	-	-			

history was to show, only the Junkers-Werke, meanwhile under new management, and Focke-Wulf with the Condor, managed the leap into the civilian market. After a short period as a transport aircraft, Dornier's impressive bird disappeared.

Production quantities doubtlessly showed that the RLM was right. For just one of the comparatively large bombers, which consumed a great deal of materials, two or three medium bombers could be built. In view of the situation at that time, it was an appropriate and even indisputable decision. The large bomber idea appeared to have been buried with General Walter Wever, but in fact it was not. The He 177 had been tailored to meet this need, but due to numerous deficiencies, caused by the RLM requirement for it to be capable of dive-bombing and powered by coupled engines, the aircraft could not fulfil its functions in the way that was demanded.

As regards the technical description of the Do 19, its all-metal semi-monocoque fuselage was of rectangular cross-section, had an over-all length of 25.50m (83ft 8in), and a basic structure of 51 transverse frames. The nose section featured glazing at the front and along the fuselage sides; later photographs reveal a ventral pannier beneath the originally slab-sided underfuselage nose section. Consisting of four sections, the fuselage was covered with smooth sheet skinning. The four separate components were joined at the nose ahead of the cockpit, ahead of the main spar well aft of the cockpit, and behind the wing auxiliary spar. The fuselage rear supported the large-area

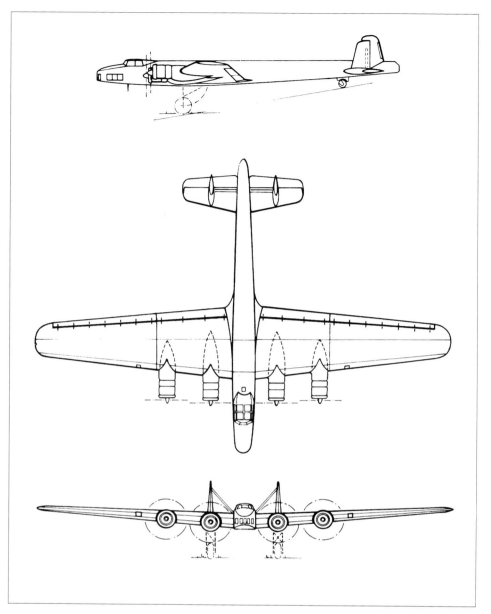

Three-view of the Dornier Do 19 V1 strategic bomber.

empennage surfaces, which comprised twin fins and rudders mounted on the two-spar tailplane and attached by auxiliary struts to the fuselage. The rudders were fabric-covered, and the tailplane could be adjusted in flight. The elevators could be moved in the range 28° up to 24° down, the figure for the rudders being 24° to either side.

The trapezoidal wing had a span of 35m (114ft 8in) and thus corresponded dimensionally to the Ju 89. Built in three sections, the two-spar structure had an area of 162m² (1,743.71ft²). The trailing-edge control surfaces, in the form of ailerons, slotted ailerons and landing flaps, stretched over the entire span of the wing, which supported the four Bramo 322 engines, each of 715hp driving a three-bladed VDM airscrew of 3.70m (12ft 1⅜in) diameter. The fuel was held in two so-called

'Cottenid' tanks, each of 1,750 litres capacity and bulletproof.

Each of the mainwheels, of 5.70m (18ft 4⅜in) track, retracted rearwards into the wheelbays behind the extended inner engine nacelles that were enclosed by streamlined nacelle door coverings. A single tailwheel was located at the rear.

To the equipped weight of 11,940kg (26,323 lb) was added 2,625kg (5,787 lb) of fuel, 290kg (639 lb) of lubricant, 700kg (1,543 lb) for the crew of seven, and a 2,945kg (6,493 lb) payload, giving a maximum take-off weight of 18,500kg (40,785 lb) and wing loading of 114.2kg/m² (23.39 lb/ft²). Maximum speed at sea-level was 315km/h (195mph), cruising speed 250km/h (155mph), range 1,540km (957 miles), and service ceiling 5,600m (18,375ft).

To conclude this description of the Ju 89 and Do 19, the table on the previous page provides a comparison with the principal designs of American origin.

Chapter Three

Transformation

From Bird of Prey to Dove

Der Große Dessauer (The Mighty Dessauer)

As already mentioned, the first Ju 90 V1 civil-use prototype was derived from the Ju 89 V3 bomber. The parallel development of civil and military versions of an aircraft was not unusual in those days, examples being provided by the Do 17, Ju 86 and He 111. (The latter is described as a separate title published in the series *From Original to Model* by Bernard & Graefe Verlag, it is to be the subject of a *Black Cross* volume published by Midland Publishing in 2004.)

The Werknummer 4913 applied to the Ju 89 V3 and the Ju 90 V1. This large transport aircraft, as it was now called, differed from the bomber configuration in several respects. The most obvious difference lay in the considerably more voluminous fuselage, which contained far more space than the Ju 89 bomber. Additionally, the powerplants in the Ju 90 V1 were DB 600Cs, but because these units were associated with its use in military projects, subsequent aircraft were powered by the BMW 132. Finally, the wing and tail surfaces were taken over from the Ju 89.

Flight Trials: Testing a Giant

The *Große Dessauer* raised itself into the air for the first time on 28th August 1937, followed by a long period of flight-testing by both manufacturer and by Lufthansa, during which 100 hours of testing were planned. This testing phase included the dangerous 'flutter' tests, which involved oscillations induced by vibration exciters that affected the wing and tail surfaces; only in this way was it possible to determine the strength of the design. In the course of such tests, on 7th February 1938, a catastrophe occurred. The programme's test pilot, Flugkapitän Karl-Heinz Kindermann, flew the Ju 90 V1 (D-AALU) during initial flights at 400km/h (249mph) without experiencing any tendency to flutter. This speed was, however, exceeded on its second flight, when several airframe components immediately displayed signs of flutter. Switching off the specially installed vibration inducer should have immediately resulted in cessation and normalisation of flying conditions, but a technical defect prevented the apparatus from shutting down, and it was only after the V1 had shed some of its parts that Kindermann and his crew decided to abandon the aircraft and save themselves by parachute. The test pilot and his flight-test engineer, Erich Gast, successfully accomplished this, but the third crew member, flight-test engineer Alfred Hahnemann, crashed to his death with the prototype. This was indeed a black day, but fortunately it had no consequences for the continuation of the programme.

This size comparison between man and machine shows the justification for the selection of the name *Der Große Dessauer*.

Left: **The 'face' of *Der Große Dessauer*.**

Above: ***Der Große Dessauer* photographed from an unusual perspective. Clearly visible are the dorsal air exhaust vents along the fuselage.**

Below left: **The Ju 90 V1 was originally scheduled to be built as the Ju 89 V3.**

Below: **The Ju 90 V1 accomplished its maiden flight on 28th August 1937.**

Press Reaction: The Ju 90 in the News

Articles published in various newspapers and aviation monthlies show how the press reacted to the new aircraft. On 18 September 1937 the *Münchner Neueste Nachrichten* (Munich Latest News) reported

40 Passengers in 'Der Große Dessauer'

'In an untiring design and manufacturing time lasting a year and a half, the largest German civilian transport aircraft, the Ju 90, was completed. It was first flight-tested a few days ago and at midday on Friday was exhibited to mem-

bers of the German press. The progress of this aircraft, in comparison with the excellent and world-acclaimed German aircraft of the past, is unique. The German aircraft industry can be justifiably proud of the creation and completion of this superb product. Its performance is an achievement for German air traffic, for its passengers, and for the high repute of German aviation throughout the world. The results of this performance will soon become visible. The new Junkers Ju 90 Großflugzeug [large aircraft], which offers 40 passengers the most comfortable space, will already form a part of the Lufthansa fleet at the beginning of next year, and come into use particularly on the

much frequented Berlin-Rome, Berlin-London, and Berlin-Paris long-distance routes. Its large capacity will be urgently required especially on these routes, since the growth of German air traffic has been so enormous during the last ten months, that on several of the routes in Germany, instead of the scheduled single flight, two additional aircraft had to be employed in order to fulfil the needs of the flying public. In the National Socialist Reich, German air traffic has attained a unique peak without, however, having reached the limit of development.

'It is almost self-understood that the new Ju 90 has been based on the great tradition of Junkers aircraft, incorporating the latest technical knowledge and experience. The manufacture of this four-engined large aircraft christened in the Junkers-Werke as "Der Große Dessauer", presented no novel technical problem, since the well-known G 38 has already been in service for several years, offering space for 30 passengers at a speed of 200km/h [124mph] but which is insufficient to meet the needs of the future. In addition, the proven Ju 52 that is flying with the greatest safety in current-day German civilian air traffic routes, will be superseded in speed by the much larger Ju 90. With its four engines, this new aircraft will have a cruising speed of 350km/h [217mph] and a maximum speed of 420km/h [261mph]…'

As one reads these lines, one can imagine that this enthusiastic author had his desk in Dessau.

Luftwissen's February 1938 edition contained the following:

About the accident to the Ju 90 D-AALU

'On the 7th of February this year, after attaining a speed of 475km/h [295mph] during flight trials with a Ju 90 prototype with artificially induced vibrations without any problems having being experienced, the series of tests was continued on the following day. At the conclusion of the flight trials and for determination of the stress limits during the latest test flight, the vibrations with the aid of an artificial device were again induced at a speed of 500km/h [310mph]. Due to failure of the vibration control apparatus, it became impossible to dampen these in time, resulting in a flight condition that caused the crew to leave the aircraft with their parachutes. Unfortunately, one of the crew members (Flight-Test Engineer Hahnemann) fell to his death because his parachute did not open in time.'

Interavia No 516, February 1938 reported:

Germany: The Ju 90 Accident
Technology and Industry

'…Unfortunately, one crew member, the Flight-Test Engineer Hahnemann, died due to his parachute failing to open in sufficient time. The aircraft was destroyed – this according to the German announcement. It is awaited with interest what consequences will be drawn by German authorities from this regrettable accident and whether they will pursue such tests on an aircraft in flight involving personnel and materiel. The official regulations certainly include flight trials at overspeeds, but not with auxiliary artificial oscillation generators. Tests of this nature on an aircraft in flight (whose significance for large aircraft is important) have been systematically carried out by the Junkerswerke for several years, by which means in practical operation, all possible agitative forces such as wind-gusts or vibrations caused by the powerplants are imitated and their influence on the entire flight speed regime are investigated.'

On 3rd July 1938 an unknown but poetic press source described an:

Interesting Flying Meet in Budaörs, Hungary
Demonstration of the Largest European Civil Aircraft

'A tiny spot grows out of the ether; it becomes winged. Soon it will become a swallow, and out of the swallow, an eagle forms. Only his powerful widespread soothing wings are perceived as he rises approaching noiselessly in the atmosphere. The large bird suddenly wrenches itself from the sea of blue; it becomes larger and larger, its four three-bladed propellers glistening blindingly. Its engines continue to roar, and then it lets down for the landing. The revolutions of the throttled motors become reduced, the pilot lets down the undercarriage at the press of a button, and now he settles down elegantly on the ground. Once again his four engines burst into a roar, as though the flying giant is offering a greeting to mother Earth, under whose laws it always remains subordinate, and then there appears above the enclosed pilot's cabin like a cross, the yellow-striped blue company flag of Deutsche Lufthansa. "Der Große Dessauer" Junkers 90 is carrying 42 passengers, consisting this time of German Reich Press representatives from Vienna and Berlin, guided by the sure hands of its Flugkapitän [Robert] Untucht, experienced on many of the world's flying routes, and now heartily welcomed in Budapest.

'Before we had in fact advanced this far, another giant butterfly appeared, flying on a direct approach and in the field of view of the excitedly awaiting guests. To them also it divulged only the shimmering motors of the three-bladed propellers. Gradually, the familiar working music of the quadruple 720hp transmitted from the mighty engine nacelles came closer. The low humming turns into tumultuous thunder, and now the two overlarge human-filled birds meet in the air and describe the most wonderful figures with such an ease and manoeuvrability as though they were nature's creatures in their element. Both of the large-capacity civil aircraft – the "Junkers 90" and the "Focke-Wulf 200" are the largest of their kind, a few of which Deutsche Lufthansa has put into operation for carrying passengers on regular airline routes. The Focke-Wulf "Condor" is piloted by yet another world-famous Chefpilot of the German airline, Graf [Siegfried] Schack, who brought it to Budapest. Accompanying him were Messrs Junge, Haberstolz, Koch and Stieda from the technical and commercial Flugleitung [Flight Operations] of the aircraft company in Bremen on a day visit, and will be received and greeted in a comradely manner here by the Hungarian Aviation Ministry with Oberdirektor Feketehalmy-Czeydner at the head of his delegation, and by Direktor Seelemann of the Budapest General Representation of the Reichsbahnzentrale [German Railways Headquarters] on behalf of German traffic public relations, and Mr Winter of Lufthansa Flight Operations in Budapest.

'For the first time, Lufthansa has introduced both of these large airliners, which had previously been tested for their technical characteristics and flying capabilities on innumerable world routes, into their summer flight plan. Both are fast passenger-carrying aircraft having a cruising speed of 350km/h [217mph], so that for the flight from Berlin-Tempelhof to Budapest-Budaörs, not much more than 2 hours have been necessary. The fact that Germany was the winner of the second international Oasis Flight in February 1937, the British London to Isle of Man Air Race in May 1937 and the Hoggarflug in January that year, is living proof of the high-performance capability of German aircraft, to which must be added that the Ju 90 Großflugzeug, piloted by the Junkerswerke Chief Test Pilot Flugkapitän Kindermann, with a payload of 5,000kg [11,023 lb] reached a world record height of 9,312m [30,551ft] – a performance that has to be rated even higher, since the flying weight of the machine alone is 20 tonnes [44,092 lb] and the calculated ceiling only 6,400m [21,000ft].

'On its test flight on the Berlin-Cairo stretch, the Focke-Wulf "Condor" achieved a world's best time of 11 hours, and for the Berlin-Lisbon stretch needs only a day's flying time for the 2,650km [1,647 miles]. Thus, both aircraft represent means of transportation that in their technical perfection are milestones of modern developments in air travel. In the Ju 90, 42 passengers are comfortably accommodated on upholstered seats, and from the Mitropa kitchen, are looked after by agile and no less pretty Stewardesses with food and drink. Over and above this, these young ladies possess an exquisite tact to becalm those passengers who tend to show signs of fear. A few minutes of diversionary conversation seem to work wonders in this regard. As the Stewardesses have confidentially reported, it is mainly the male passengers who have the need for a few words of calm and encouragement. The motto of the Ju 90 is: It flies itself! By this is meant that the aircraft possesses characteristics which enable it, with hands off the controls, to remain in stable flight and even take corrective action in wind gusts. By this means, the possibility has now been created to adhere 100 per cent to a flight timetable in all types of weather conditions. In terms of internal cabin furnishings, nothing has been left out for passenger comfort. Each traveller in the Focke-Wulf aircraft has a headrest and seat arm supports, a reading lamp, ashtray, cigarette lighter, a bell-button to summon the Stewardess and other frills for the traveller's well-being. The invited journalists then ascend on the wings of the German Lufthansa for a round trip over Budapest, and beneath them view the multifarious picture of

On the Ju 90 V1 the airspeed measurement probe was mounted on the starboard wing.

The Ju 90 V1 was finished in Hellgrau (bright grey), the engine nacelles in black.

All of the aircraft's markings were in black.

Photograph on the opposite page:

The national insignia on the endplate fins and rudders consisted of a red band enclosing the black swastika in a white disc.

our magnificent capital with its surrounding garland of mountains and the unending plains that disappear immeasurably eastwards.

'A splendid ivory-coloured Savoia Marchetti SM 75 machine for use on the route between Prague and Warsaw completes the fairy-tale picture of the conquest of the air by mankind...'

A month earlier, on 7th June 1938, the *Berliner Illustrierte Nachtausgabe* (Berlin Illustrated Night Edition), had described:

Grosser Dessauer 9,312m high

'...The record flight of the "Große Dessauer" took place from Dessau airfield. The Junkers-Werke Chefpilot Flugkapitän Kindermann, co-pilot [Flugkapitän Rupprecht] Wendel and Flight-Test Engineer Hopf [his name was actually Werner Hotopf] exceeded the previous record of 8,980m [29,462ft] that had been set up abroad, by more than 300m [984ft]. The "Große Dessauer" is likewise powered by four Daimler-Benz engines. The Reichsminister for Aviation and Commander-in-Chief of the Luftwaffe, Generalfeldmarschall Göring, expressed his special recognition to the German record crew for their superb performance and equally to the aircraft company.'

On 2nd August 1939, one month before the outbreak of the Second World War, the following account appeared in the *Mittelschlesische Gebirgszeitung* (Central Silesian Highland Newspaper), Waldenburg:

Ju 90 – The London Sensation

'On Tuesday, the new German 20-tonne passenger aircraft, the Ju 90 "Mecklenburg", with a crew of four, landed in London for the first time. As the British press has particularly emphasised, it is luxuriously equipped for 40 passengers. The Berlin-Amsterdam-London route was accomplished in four hours. The new German giant aircraft, which, as the largest landplane in the world, has caused noticeable excitement in England, is from now on to operate on the Berlin-London route on a daily service, and will certainly contribute to provide a boost to the interest in further British circles for tourist traffic with Germany...'

The author of the article then continued in a significantly different tone. Although not directly relevant, the passage is nevertheless of interest as it represents the typical tone of the press at that time: 'In the British public domain, it has evoked attention that 400 visas and more are issued daily for Britons who travel to Germany. The "Daily Mail" has emphasised the fact that while the older generation fought against Germany, thousands of young Britons have made up their minds to visit that country. As we ourselves hear, it is a fact that precisely in the circles of workers and employees, small businessmen and students, a strong urge is visible that in itself forms a judgement of Germany. Even groups of sportsmen and sportswomen have not allowed themselves to be

deterred by the agitation against Germany, to travel and partake in German sporting events despite the attention of the Press and the enemies of Germany directed against them. Without overestimating such symptoms, it can nevertheless be confirmed that reasonable and calmly thinking circles in Britain do not allow themselves to be throttled by Jewish hate politics and insist on forming their own opinions.' And so on...

'Guinea Pigs': The Ju 90 V2 to V13 Prototypes

Ju 90 V2

This, the second in the series of prototypes, Werknummer 4914, civil registration D-AIVI, accomplished its maiden flight on 2nd December 1937. Flight trials of this aircraft also ended in an enormous disaster.

In terms of technical detail, the V2 displayed considerable alterations. The entire propulsion system, which on the V1 featured the DB 600, was replaced by the air-cooled BMW 132 radial, a development step that was accompanied by several initial difficulties. A further alteration was made to the empennage surfaces. In the course of its flight-test programme, the aircraft was stationed from 11th May 1938 in Rechlin, and subsequently entered the planned 100-hour series of tests (from 26th May) by Lufthansa. The *Preussen* (Prussia), as it had been christened by DLH, gave good results,

vapours. Thus a combination of technical and human shortcomings were now leading towards disaster. Shortly after take-off, the BMW 132 engine concerned drastically lost power, with the result that the aircraft slewed to port from the runway and sliced through the sole palm tree situated on that side some 170 metres (560 feet) away, whereupon fire broke out. With the exception of four Junkers employees, all others aboard perished.

Two crashes within a relatively short period of time did not strengthen the reputation of the Ju 90, and still less that of the Junkers-Werke. In addition to the already cited factors, the Investigation Committee established yet another cause: reduced effectiveness of the ailerons and rudder had further contributed to the catastrophe, which now took on a greater importance during the flight trials of subsequent prototypes.

Ju 90 V3

The third prototype, Werknummer 4915, registration D-AURE, and initially christened by DLH as *Württemberg*, took off on its maiden flight on 23rd June 1938, and appeared in the DLH inventory the following month. Later rechristened *Bayern* (Bavaria), the aircraft commenced route testing, taking into account all of the knowledge gained during evaluation of the crash of its forbear and the improvements that resulted. On 31st July Lufthansa introduced *Bayern* on its Munich-Berlin-Frankfurt-Berlin-Munich route, on 28th August it made its appearance in Stockholm, and on 23rd September in Helsinki. Its further use included, among others, special duties as a transport for the wartime German-French Weapons Ceasefire Commission. In August 1944 it became the victim of an Allied bombing raid.

Ju 90 V4

In this configuration, the V4 represented the prototype of a subsequent mini-series (of ten aircraft). It initially served as a test aircraft at Junkers, later being taken over by the Luftwaffe as a transport. It survived the war, and in May 1945 became an Allied war trophy.

The Ju 90 V4, Werknummer 4916, D-ADLH, flew for the first time on 12th September 1938. It entered Lufthansa service on 8th November, and was christened *Schwabenland* (Swabia). Alterations made to this prototype included an outer wing dihedral reduced to 3° (as opposed to the 6.5° of the V3) and a third vertical fin and rudder, which was to have optimised flight stability. Only the first-named modification to the V3 was retained on all subsequent prototypes.

The table at the top of page 34 lists all the V-models that appeared during the course of development of this aircraft. The Ju 90 V1 to V4 were purely civil-use examples, while the V5 served as the prototype of the military models.

fully confirmed later in acceptance flights conducted by Director Karl August von Gablenz.

Following the completion of testing, the Ju 90 was fitted out with comfortable internal furnishings in addition to the on-board kitchen. The next and last phase in the life of the *Preussen* began with the flight in stages from Dessau to South America, a distance of several thousand kilometres in stretches of uninterrupted flight, intended to show the world that the Ju 90 was capable of flying long distances as well as being reliable under tropical conditions. The crew for this undertaking was made up of pilots Robert Untucht and Joachim Blankenburg, radio operators Kurt Gillwald and Theodor Sager, and the Junkers flight mechanic, Heinrich Lardong. Further individuals on board were recruited from BMW, Junkers, and RLM personnel. On 21st November 1938 D-AIVI lifted off from Dessau and departed in the direction of Marseilles on the first stage of the journey. The second stage took it to Africa, via Las Palmas and Dakar to

Bathurst, Gambia, where catastrophe struck, due to a combination of technological shortcomings and a measure of over-confidence and lack of consideration for local conditions.

On the morning of 26th November 1938 the *Preussen* took off from Dakar towards Bathurst, a destination that was merely intended as an 'excursion'. The Ju 90 V2 headed inland and landed at around 1100 hours in Bathurst. Because of the lack of a protective hangar, the aircraft was parked in the burning sun of Africa until the afternoon, and the immense heat caused unnoticed pockets of vapour to develop in the fuel conduits of the port outer engine. At 1630 hours the aircraft taxied for take-off, the crew unaware of any danger. According to the testimony of surviving Junkers personnel, the usual slowing down of the engines was dispensed with prior to take-off, as well as the switching on of the auxiliary fuel pumps, specially installed to guarantee the fuel supply under extreme conditions, which would have countered the build-up of the deadly fuel

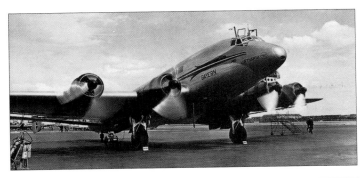

Top left: **Loading the Ju 90 V3 *Württemberg* with luggage and mail.**

Top right: **The uniformed individual near *Württemberg* does not belong to German Railways, but is a member of the so-called 'Air Police' force.**

Upper left: **A picture of *Württemberg* in the heyday of Lufthansa, which came to a sad end due to the war.**

Upper right: **Bayern (Bavaria) runs up its BMW 132 engines to operating temperature. In the background is the Ju 90 V2 D-AIVI *Preussen* (Prussia).**

Lower left: **Bayern seen from another perspective. The lettering and the DLH Kranich (Crane) emblem were in black.**

Lower right: **D-AURE Bayern had a silver 'outfit' with black engine nacelles. The fins were painted with a red band and black swastika inside a white disc.**

Bottom left: **The Ju 90 D-ABDG, also christened *Württemberg*, was taken on by Lufthansa on 4th May 1939.**

Bottom right: **Only two weeks later, Lufthansa added the Ju 90Z-2 D-ADFJ Baden, Werknummer 900003, to its inventory.**

Aircraft of the Ju 90 / Ju 290 Experimental Programme

Ju 90	Werknummer	First flight	Civil Reg	Luftwaffe Registration	Remarks
V1	4913	28.08.1937	D-AALU	-	*Der Große Dessauer.* Crashed 06.02.1938 during test flight.
V2	4914	02.12.1937	D-AIVI	-	DLH *Preussen,* ex-*Sachsen.* Crashed 26.11.38 at Bathurst, Gambia.
V3	4915	23.06.1938	D-AURE	GF + GD	DLH *Bayern,* ex-*Württemberg.* Flight tests at Junkers-Werke. Used on special missions. Destroyed on 09.08.1944 in Allied bombing raid.
V4	4916	12.09.1938	D-ADLH	KH + XA, J4 + DH, G6 + BY	DLH *Sachsen,* ex-*Schwabenland.* Initially part of a test programme at Junkers, then used militarily. Scrapped in UK as war trophy.
V5	4917	05.12.1939	D-ANBS	KH + XB	Initially used by Junkers on air-towing trials. Transport and works flights until winter 1943. Test aircraft for wing suction system.
V6	4918	30.07.1940	D-AOKD	-	Junkers test aircraft. Fuselage later used for manufacture of Ju 390 V1.
V7	4919	06.09.1941	D-APFH	GF + GH, J4 + CH, G6 + AY	Used by Luftwaffe as Transport. Set on fire following undercarriage damage on 5.10.44 near Athens. Wrongly described, like the V8, as Ju 90 S.
V8	4920	28.03.1942	D-AQJA	DJ + YE, J4 + BH	Transport flights in Mediterranean. Taken out of use following undercarriage damage on 19.8.43 Similar to V7; represented transition to Ju 290.
V9	-	-	-	-	Construction order for this civilian prototype cancelled 20.10.39. Had 12 window rows, and BMW 801, Jumo 213, Jumo 209 engines. Fuselage was probably under construction
V10	-	-	-	-	Construction order for this military prototype cancelled 20.10.39. Fuselage was most probably also under construction. If so, V9/V10 fuselages would have found use in Ju 290 production. Intended powerplants were BMW 801 or Jumo 213
V11	ex-srs 900011	-	-	-	Prototype of Ju 90A-1 Transport. Served later for completion of Ju 290 V1 prototype.
V12	ex-srs 900001	24.02.1939	D-ABDG	GF + GB	DLH *Württemberg.* Used by Luftwaffe as weapons test carrier. Returned to DLH and became war booty 24.4.45.
V13	ex-srs 900012	-	-	-	Originally prototype of Ju 90A-1, then Ju 290 V2. Completed as Werknummer 290 110 151.

Technical Data Comparisons Between the Ju 89, Ju 90 V3, Ju 90Z-3 (SAA) and Ju 290 V1

	Ju 89	Ju 90 V3	Ju 90Z-3 (SAA*)	Ju 290 V1
Powerplants	Daimler-Benz 600C	BMW 132H1	Pratt & Whitney Twin Wasp	BMW 801A
Take-off power, hp	910	830	1,200	1,560
Wingspan	35.00m (114' 10")	35.30m (115' 9¾")	35.30m (115' 9¾")	42.00m (137' 9½")
Length	26.30m (86' 3½")	26.45m (86' 9⅜")	26.45m (86' 9⅜")	26.68m (87' 6⅜")
Height	6.50m (21' 3⅞")	7.05m (23' 1½")	7.05m (23' 1½")	7.02m (23' 0⅜")
Wing area, m² (ft²)	184.0 (1,980.5)	184.0 (1,980.5)	184.0 (1,980.5)	203.6 (2,191.5)
Equipped weight, kg (lb)	16,000 (35,274)	16,500 (36,376)	16,535 (36,453)	20,860 (45,988)
Fuel weight, kg (lb)	3,000 (6,614)	2,500 (5,512)	3,130 (6,900)	10,200 (22,487)
Take-off weight (max), kg (lb)	27,800 (61,288)	23,300 (51,367)	25,800 (56,879)	40,500 (89,286)
Max speed, km/h (mph)	410 (255)	350 (217)	380 (236)	424 (263)
Cruising speed, km/h (mph)	310 (193)	320 (199)	325 (202)	356 (221)
Range, km (miles)	2,980 (1,852)	1,540 (957)	2,080 (1,292)	4,000 (2,486)
Landing speed, km/h (mph)	110 (68.4)	109 (67.7)	110 (68.4)	124 (77)
Passengers/crew	-/5	40/4	40/4	48/5†

* South African Airways; † Payload 6,500kg (14,330 lb)

A rear view of *Bayern*. The black letters D-AURE can be seen on the upper side of the wings.

Chapter Four

New Dimensions in Air Travel

German Aircraft Comparable to the Ju 90

Focke-Wulf Fw 200 Condor

Towards the middle of the 1930s a new aircraft in Germany was to make its appearance – the Focke-Wulf Condor – bringing together an elegance and performance that overshadowed anything that engineering design had previously been able to combine. Even the name for his four-engined aircraft – the majestic bird of the Andes mountains – had been held in readiness by its Focke-Wulf designer and test pilot Dipl.-Ing. Kurt Tank, and was soon to be on everyone's lips. But first, Kurt Tank and his team had a lot of design work to undertake. The airliner had a long, slim fuselage laid out to accommodate 20 passengers, a trapezoidal wing planform of high-aspect ratio, and four powerplants. Tank's argument that the technical possibilities were already sufficiently far advanced to be able to consider such a project was shared by Lufthansa. One of the main reasons for these deliberations was the extended routes to Africa and South America; these were operated by flying-boats served by catapult-equipped ships, so an important cost factor could be considerably reduced using a suitably designed landplane.

As early as June 1936 the project passed from outline design to a firm construction order, and it was only through the supreme organisation and effort of those involved on the project that this had been possible. The result of this hectic period stood ready for its maiden flight on 27th July 1937. Powered by the roar of four American Pratt & Whitney Hornet radials, the Fw 200 V1 (at this time bearing the civil regis-

The Focke-Wulf Fw 200 Condor was an elegant rival – this is D-AMHC *Nordmark*.

tration D-AERE) lifted off into its natural element. A flight of only a short duration was sufficient to demonstrate the absolutely solid qualities of this new airliner.

In order to make his Condor known throughout the world, Kurt Tank decided to conduct a long-distance flight with journalists on board. His aim was to cover the Berlin-Cairo-Berlin route within 24 hours, which, if successfully accomplished, would certainly have a very positive effect the order-books. It was decided, accordingly, to utilise the power of the press.

However, the African episode represented only a 'small excursion'. Now, the Condor was to conquer the Atlantic, as dozens of pioneers had attempted in years gone by, to make the

big leap over the Großen Teich (Large Pond). The Junkers W 33 *Bremen* had already flown the east-west route to land at Labrador, but the destination now was not to be a deserted location, but New York itself, then the focal point of international travel by sea, followed, possibly soon afterwards, by offering extensive connections by air. The honour of carrying out the planned record flight was to be accorded to the Fw 200 V1. Registered previously as D-AERE and named *Brandenburg*, to a certain extent this 'guinea-pig' example of the Condor was expected to display to the eyes of the world its qualities and the limits of technical possibilities during the course of an extreme undertaking. However, numerous preparations had to be completed first, not least of which were modifications to the aircraft itself. Where cabin space had previously been filled with comfortable cloth-covered armchairs, tables and reading lamps to ease the passengers' journeys, it was now turned to more practical use. The passenger area was converted into a fuel reservoir housing several fuel tanks on each side of the fuselage together with associated fuel lines and transfer pumps. It was through this conversion that the Condor, in the form of a 'flying fuel container', was able to make the trip across the Atlantic to the 'New World'. Together with the wing tanks, a total of 11,500 litres of fuel was available for the four thirsty engines. Upon completion of the necessary work, Flugkapitän Alfred Henke with his crew, consisting of his co-pilot Hauptmann Rudolf Freiherr von Moreau, flight mechanic Paul Dierberg and radio operator Walter Kober, were able to devote themselves to completing the final preparations.

On the evening of 10th August 1938, a good ten years after the flight of the *Bremen*, and loaded with an enormous quantity of fuel, the Condor stood ready on the airfield at Berlin-Staaken. Like the proverbial 'leaden duck' it rose from the runway and slowly but surely gained height on a course to the west. The time was precisely 2005 hours Central European Time. The crew were required to report their position every hour to the Hamburg Overseas Radio Station at Quickborn. Hamburg, the 'gateway to the world', was overflown at 2055 hours. Three hours later, Kober reported his position over the British Isles near Glasgow. Finally, the Condor left British territory behind and levelled off at a height of 2,000 metres (6,560 feet) to conquer the long, dangerous and relatively most monotonous stretch of the flight.

During 1938/39, Lufthansa placed a total of 12 Condors in service. Pictured here is D-AXFO *Pommern* (Pomerania).

D-AETA *Westfalen* (Westphalia) runs up its BMW 132 engines. The Fw 200 also had the capability of an engine quick-change.

Another view of the clear lines of the Fw 200, as exemplified by the D-AETA *Westfalen*.

Finally, after what seemed like endless hours, the watery 'desert' of the Atlantic had been crossed, and the weary crew sighted Newfoundland; in Europe the time was 1400 hours. The most important and risky part of the undertaking was now behind them, but the crew still faced a number of hours ahead across the North American continent until they reached New York. At 2041 hours European Time the Quickborn station received the reassuring news: 'Arrived in New York'. On the way there the Condor had been accompanied by several aircraft chartered by the American press. Considerably more elegant, and thousands of kilogrammes lighter, the machine descended to land at the local Floyd Bennett airfield. With a respectable 1,000 litres of fuel still remaining, Henke set down D-ACON and taxied to the allocated parking apron. The revolutions of the noisy motors ceased – they had done it!

On 13th August Henke and his crew headed back for home. Because there was no headwind – a factor that had made the outward crossing so difficult – the return journey was quicker, at 19 hours and 55 minutes. An enthusiastic reception at Berlin-Tempelhof greeted them, and the undertaking was crowned with an FAI-recognised Long-Distance Record – the bridge between Europe and the New World had been flown at an average speed of 321km/h (199.5mph) over the then breathtaking distance of 6,371km (3,959 miles).

A three-view drawing of the Fw 200.

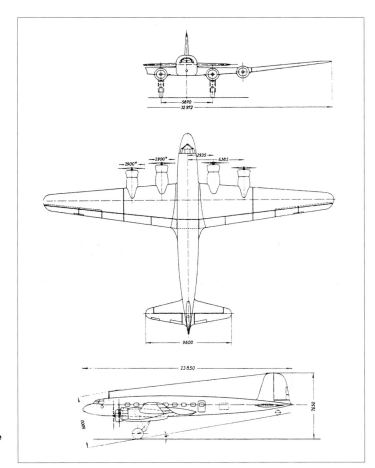

A sectional view of the structural features of the Condor.

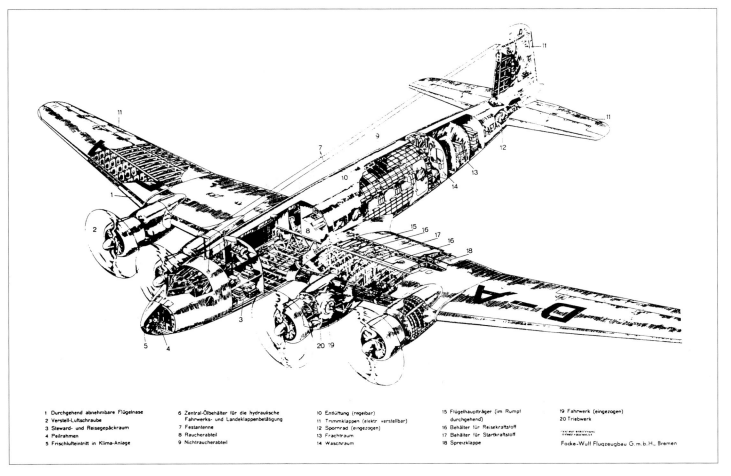

1 Durchgehend abnehmbare Flügelnase
2 Verstell-Luftschraube
3 Steward- und Reisegepäckraum
4 Peilrahmen
5 Frischlufteintritt in Klima-Anlage
6 Zentral-Ölbehälter für die hydraulische Fahrwerks- und Landeklappenbetätigung
7 Festantenne
8 Raucherabteil
9 Nichtraucherabteil
10 Entlüftung (regelbar)
11 Trimmklappen (elektr. verstellbar)
12 Spornrad (eingezogen)
13 Frachtraum
14 Waschraum
15 Flügelhauptträger (im Rumpf durchgehend)
16 Behälter für Reisekraftstoff
17 Behälter für Startkraftstoff
18 Spreizklappe
19 Fahrwerk (eingezogen)
20 Triebwerk

Focke-Wulf Flugzeugbau G.m.b.H., Bremen

Technical Data of the Focke-Wulf Fw 200 Condor

Aircraft	Fw 200 V1 (D-AERE)	Fw 200 (D-ACON)	V1 Fw 200A-0	Fw 200B-1
Powerplants (4)	Pratt & Whitney Hornet	BMW 132L	BMW 132L	BMW 132Dc
Take-off power, hp	760	800	800	850
Propellers	two-bladed	two-bladed	two-bladed	two-bladed
Wingspan	32.84m* (107' 8⅞")	32.84m (107' 8⅞")	32.84m (107' 8⅞")	32.84m (107' 8⅞")
Length	23.85m (78' 3")	23.85m (78' 3")	23.85m (78' 3")	23.85m (78' 3")
Height	6.00m (19' 8¼")	6.00m (19' 8¼")	6.00m (19' 8¼")	6.00m (19' 8¼")
Wing area, m^2 (ft^2)	118* (1,270.1)	118* (1,270.1)	118* (1,270.1)	118* (1,270.1)
Equipped weight, kg (lb)	9,200 (20,282)	8,800 (19,400)	10,925 (24,085)	11,300 (24,912)
Fuel weight (max), kg (lb)	2,520 (5,556)	11,500 (25,353)	2,600 (5,732)	3,700 (8,157)
Lubricant weight, kg (lb)	200 (441)	450 (992)	280 (617)	280 (617)
Take-off weight, kb (lb)	14,000 (30,864)	21,200 (46,737)	17,000 (37,478)	17,000 (37,478)
Wing loading at take-off, kg/m^2 (lb/ft^2)	118.6 (24.3)	179.7 (36.8)	144.1 (29.5)	144.1 (29.5)
Max speed, km/h (mph)	375 (233)	310 (193)	340 (211)	376 (234)
Cruising speed, km/h (mph)	355 (221)	280 (174)	325 (202)	365 (227)
at altitude, m (ft)	1,000 (3,280)	1,000 (3,280)	1,000 (3,280)	3,000 (9,840)
Range (normal), km (miles)	1,250 (777)	-	1,250 (777)	1,500 (932)
Range (max), km (miles)	-	6,500 (4,039)	1,700 (1,056)	2,000 (1,243)
Service ceiling, m (ft)	6,100m (20,015ft)	3,000m (9,840ft)	6,000m (19,685ft)	7,200m (23,620ft)
Passengers/crew	26/4	–/4	26/4	26/4

* Original span was 32.97m (108ft) and wing area 120m^2 (1,291.6ft^2)

As a result of this superb American flight, a record attempt to far-off Japan was now put in progress. Some three and a half months after the flight to New York, at 1555 hours Central European Time on 28th November D-ACON rose from the runway at Berlin-Tempelhof destined for Tokyo. The crew were the same as that on the August flight, accompanied this time by aircraft mechanic Georg Kohne and sales director Heinz Junge, both of Focke-Wulf. In all, four stages were planned. The outbound flight turned out to be completely problem-free, accomplished by Henke and his crew in 46 hours 18 minutes, of which 4 hours 18 minutes was spent refuelling, in order to achieve the journey of 13,844km (8,602 miles). So far so good, but problems arose during the return flight. Suddenly two engines on the same side began to cough, and shortly afterwards failed completely. What followed was a series of misassessments of the situation and consequential false reactions, resulting in an unnecessary ditching in shallow water in the Bay of Manila. The reason for the loss of both engines had been incorrect fuel tank switching.

However, turning from these spectacular events to routine 'airbus' services, after only a short period the Focke-Wulf order-books were filled with orders for the Condor. Lufthansa ordered ten, and two more for the South American Syndicato Condor, while two each were ordered by Denmark and Finland. In addition, construction contracts came from Japan as well as from the RLM for courier machines. A total of 16 aircraft of the civil version had been ordered in various configurations, and these were followed by a B-series that featured a more robust undercarriage with twin mainwheels, an altered engine cowling and a smaller rudder area.

Two of these aircraft, transferred to the Syndicato Condor and denoted by an asterisk in table at the bottom of this page, were registered there under the Brazilian registrations PP-CBI *Abaitara* (formerly D-AXFO) and PP-CBJ *Arumani* (formerly D-ASBK). The other Fw 200 aircraft were equally short-lived in Lufthansa service, since during the war its Condors were also clothed in military camouflage, and only two were returned to the company. None of the former airliners employed in the rough missions conducted by the Luftwaffe survived past the year 1945. Some foreign-used examples enjoyed a brief reprieve before ending with the scrap dealer. Besides the two Brazilian examples, in 1938 two Fw 200s were sold to Denmark.

Hardly had the heyday of this pioneering aircraft begun than it ended abruptly through its military use and the consequent ad hoc development that, despite its success, was of only limited suitability to the Condor in this quite different sphere of activity. The turbulent years of the war required no airliners, but instead bomb-laden long-range reconnaissance aircraft that were able to carry their loads to distant targets or to serve, for example, as transports carrying provisions of all kinds in support of the beleaguered soldiers in Stalingrad. British Prime Minister Winston Churchill termed the Condor the 'Scourge of the Atlantic'. For armed operations, however, the Condor was only of limited use, so its success and continually new and improved bomber variations made no difference. The career of a very promising civil aircraft thus came to an end before it had been able to establish itself on a long-term basis. The Condor thus shared this destiny with the Ju 90, and it never attained the same degree of familiarity as other well-known designs of Kurt Tank.

Fw 200 Condors in Lufthansa Service

Werk-Nr	Registration	Name (prototype or series)	
2484	D-AETA	*Westfalen*	(V2)
2893	D-ADHR	*Saarland*	(V4)
2895	D-AMHC	*Nordmark*	(V5)
2994	D-ARHW	*Friesland*	(V7)
2995	D-ASBK	*Holstein**	(A-0)
2996	D-AXFO	*Pommern**	(V9)
3098	D-ACVH	*Grenzmark*	(V6)
3324	D-ABOD	*Kurmark*	(VI0)
0001	D-ACWG	*Holstein*	(B-1)
0009	D-ASHH	*Hessen*	(B-1)
0020	D-AMHL	*Pommern*	(D-2)
0021	D-ASVX	*Thüringen*	(D-2)

Focke-Wulf Fw 300 Project

Work on this optimised successor to the Fw 200 was to have been carried out in France, and design work during the war was pursued in a co-operative effort by Focke-Wulf personnel and the French SNCASO, the project headed by Dipl.-Ing. Wilhelm Bansemir. However, after two years the RLM decided to discontinue the work. This project consisted of an airliner with a capacity of 32 passengers plus a crew of five. The span was 46.80m (153ft 6½in) and the length 31.34m (102ft 9⅞in). Equipped weight was given as 27,324kg (60,238 lb), fuel weight 15,080kg (33,245 lb) for the four Jumo 222E motors, and take-off weight 47,500kg (104,719 lb). The estimated range of this variant was 7,000km (4,350 miles), the intended cabin altitude enabling the aircraft to fly at altitudes up to 11,000m (36,090ft). This 'Super Condor' was also designed in a configuration capable of transporting up to 40 passengers and containing 19,000 litres of fuel for its four DB 603 engines.

A further long-range reconnaissance project designed in 1942 was intended to solve several problems, but this likewise progresses no further than the drawing-board. In this case the span was to be 46.20m (151ft 6⅞in), length 32.20m (105ft 7¾in), take-off weight 47,500kg (104,719 lb) and range 9,000km (5,592 miles). Powerplants were four DB 603s or Jumo 222s.

The Junkers EF 100 Project

The roots of this spectacular development go back to the year 1940, when it was believed that the war was as good as won. Those responsible in the RLM as well as in Lufthansa and in industry began to reflect upon new civil aircraft that would enter post-war airline service, replacing less effective types. Activities to this end were also being undertaken in the Junkers-Werke. On the drawing-board at least there appeared a gigantic six-engined modern airliner under the designation EF 100 (EF = Entwicklungsflugzeug or Development Aircraft). Junkers at first worked out the basic design features of the aircraft and the performance calculations. Whether these values would have been confirmed in practice is not known, and it was only after the war that a start on detail design was to have been undertaken.

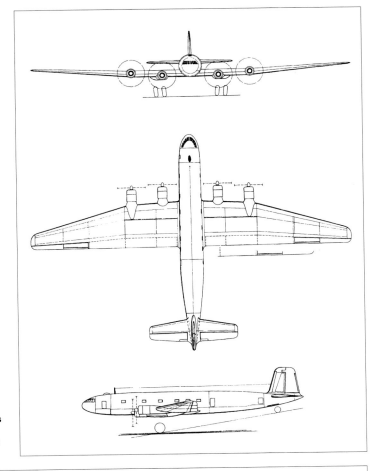

The Fw 300, which unfortunately remained only a project.

Its overall dimensions made the EF 100 an airliner of gargantuan proportions.

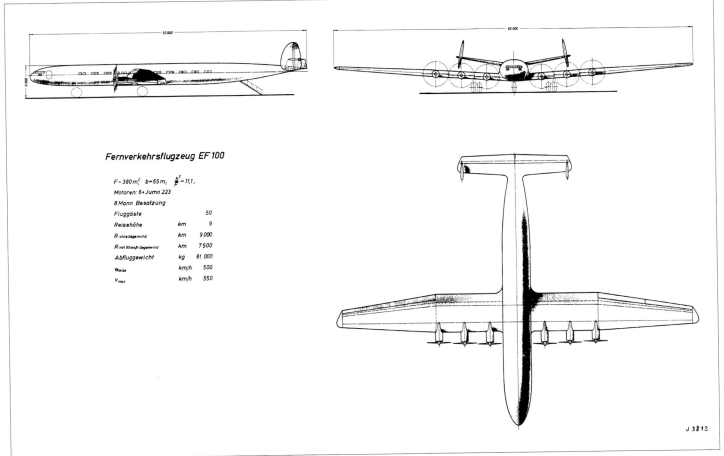

Fernverkehrsflugzeug EF 100

$F = 380\,m^2$, $b = 65\,m$, $\frac{b^2}{F} = 11,1$,

Motoren: 6 × Jumo 223

8 Mann Besatzung

Fluggäste		50
Reisehöhe	km	9
R ohne Gegenwind	km	9 000
R mit 90 km/h Gegenwind	km	7 500
Abfluggewicht	kg	81 000
V Reise	km/h	500
V max	km/h	550

Technical Data of the Junkers EF 100

Design Scheme	Ausführung I	Ausführung II
Powerplants	Jumo 223	Jumo 223
Take-off power, hp	6 x 2,500	6 x 2,500
Wingspan	65.00m (213' 3")	65.00m (213' 3")
Length	50.00m (164' 0½")	50.00m (164' 0½")
Wing area, m² (ft²)	380 (4,090.2)	380 (4,090.2)
Equipped weight, kg (lb)	44,200 (97,443)	43,900 (96,782)
Fuel weight, kg (lb)	17,400 (38,360)	27.100 (59,745)
Take-off weight, kg (lb)	74,500 (164,243)	80,500 (177,470)
Wing loading at take-off, kg/m² (lb/ft²)	196 (40.16)	212 (43.39)
Max speed, km/h (mph)	570 (354)	565 (351)
Cruising speed, km/h (mph)	545 (339)	545 (339)
Range (max), km (miles)	6,000 (3,728)	9,000 (5,592)
Service ceiling, m (ft)	12,300 (40,355)	11,600 (38,060)
Passengers/crew	72/8	50/6

The proposal catered for three design configurations:

- Transportation of 50 passengers and a range of 9,000km (5,592 miles)
- Capacity for 72 passengers and a range of 6,000km (3,728 miles)
- Capacity for a maximum of 100 passengers and a range of 4,000km (3,660 miles)

In the third configuration the capacity was thus two and a half times that of the Ju 90, which appeared dwarf-like in comparison. An aircraft with such enormous dimensions – the span was 65.00m (213ft 3in) and the length 50.00m (164ft 0¼in) – needed considerable power, intended to be supplied by six Jumo 223 24-cylinder units, providing an overall figure of no less than 15,000hp. This extraordinary motive power was based on a take-off weight in one case of 74.5 tonnes (164,243 lb) and in another 80.5 tonnes (177,470 lb). In order to provide the passengers with the best comfort at sufficient altitudes under the most favourable economic conditions, the EF 100 was to have had a pressurised cabin, a rare design feature at that time, enabling flight at up to 12,300m (40,355ft).

A section of the Junkers EF 100 fuselage.

The interior of the EF 100 was designed to offer maximum comfort.

Several projects epitomised the 'gigantomania' of the Third Reich, and the EF 100 seemed to conform; however, upon closer observation it in fact stood on 'solid ground'. It was not technical or design factors that prevented it from becoming a reality. With the EF 100, as well as smaller 'offshoots', the Junkers-Werke would have brought into being a successful family of aircraft, while co-operation among German aircraft manufacturers would have created healthy international competition. However, history and the outcome of the Second World War stifled the potential of German aviation, particularly in the civil aviation sphere; under other circumstances the dominance that the American 'Big Three' – Boeing, Douglas and Lockheed – certainly enjoyed from 1945 until the appearance of the European Airbus, would never have been so significant.

On the subject of the EF 100, the following should be mentioned: in addition to the civil design proposals, a transport as well as a long-range reconnaissance version had been worked upon. The latter took shape on the drawing-board during the period 1940-42, and had a span of 65.00m (213ft 3in), a length of 49.80m (163ft 4⅝in) and a range of 9,000km (5,592 miles), and was powered by six 24-cylinder twin-piston Jumo 223 engines with a total capacity of 28.95 litres (1,767in³). Work on the project was terminated in 1942.

The Junkers EFo-21-3 Project

Worthy of mention in this connection is yet another Junkers project whose origin on the drawing-board cannot be ascribed to a specific date. It consisted of an Atlantic aircraft bearing the designation EFo-21-3, the latter digit indicating the 3rd Entwurf (proposal). Designed to be powered by six engines, it resembled the Savoia-Marchetti airliner, except for its twin fins and rudders. Its most important features were:

- Double-decker rectangular fuselage c35.00m (114ft 10in) in length
- Trapezoidal wing planform of c44.5m (146ft) span
- Twin inset fins and rudders
- Horizontal height on ground c8.90m (29ft 2⅜in)
- A paired arrangement for the engines, which could operate independently of each other, either singly or coupled, each pair of engines driving a single set of airscrews. The type of powerplant is unknown, save for the 1,500hp given. The annular radiators, however, suggest that it may have been the Jumo 211.
- A further feature was the combination of a tailwheel with twin sets of mainwheels
- Performance calculations included a range of 6,000km (3,728 miles) and a speed of 380km/h (236mph), carrying 40 passengers and 3,400kg (7,496 lb) of mail and freight

Very similar in overall appearance were the Italian Savoia-Marchetti designs and the post-war French Breguet Provence airliners. The Br 763 Provence and its military offshoot, the Sahara, had their origins in 1944. Despite the circumstances, this design had already been drawn up at that time for an aircraft tailored to post-war civilian traffic, and with it the engineers departed from conventional guidelines as to how a future passenger or freight aircraft should look. It took five years to progress from the initial design sketches through a long period of design and construction to the ready-to-fly end product, but the aircraft finally stood ready for its maiden flight on 19th February 1949. The predecessor of the later Provence made its debut under the designation Br 761 Deux Ponts, but the clumsy-looking aircraft never attained the popularity of the American aircraft that were dominant at the time.

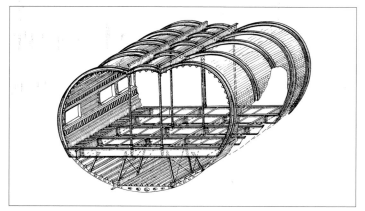

Technical Data of the Breguet Br 763 Provence

Powerplant	Pratt & Whitney
Model	R-2800-CA-18
Take-off power, hp	4 x 2,400
Airscrews	Three-blade variable-pitch
Airscrew diameter	4.22m (13' 10⅛")
Wingspan	42.99m (141' 0½")
Length	28.95m (94' 11¾")
Height	9.90m (32' 5¾")
Wing area, m² (ft²)	185.5 (1,996.66)
Empty weight, kg (lb)	34,100 (75,177)
Fuel capacity, litres	14,900
Take-off weight (max), kg (lb)	51,600 (113,757)
Wing loading at take-off, kg/m² (lb/ft²)	278.2 (57)
Max speed, km/h (mph)	425 (264)
Cruising speed, km/h (mph)	345 (214)
Landing speed, km/h (mph)	145 (90)
Range (normal), km (miles)	2,700 (1,678)
Range (max), km (miles)	3,300 (2,051)
Service ceiling, m (ft)	7,200 (15,875)
Passengers/crew	107-135/7-8

Top: As a comparison to the Junkers EFo-21-3 is the monstrous Breguet Deux Ponts, the predecessor of the Provence airliner.

Below left: **The Junkers EFo-21-3 long-range airliner project.**

Below right: **The Arado E 390 airliner project.**

The Arado E 390 Project

In 1940 the Arado Flugzeugwerke also drew up a project for a high-altitude civil transport conceived in four variants, the E 390 intended to have found use on both European as well as transatlantic routes. Design of the aircraft was undertaken between July and October 1940, the variants having a passenger capacity varying from 12 to 32, and ranges from 2,000km (1,243 miles) to 7,000km (4,350 miles). Take-off weights ranged from 24 tonnes (52,910 lb) to 28.5 tonnes (62,831 lb). All variants were to have been powered by the Jumo 208, for which 11,200 litres of fuel would have been carried.

Since it was designed with a pressurised passenger cabin, altitudes of up to 10,000m (32,810ft) were no illusion. The estimated speed was 377km/h at 6,000m (234mph at 19,685ft).

Regrettably, this interesting aircraft remained only a project, and military developments of much higher priority resulted in this airliner also being consigned to the desk-drawer. The accompanying three-view provides an impression of its configuration as well as its principal dimensions: span 29.80m (97ft 9¼in), length 24.50m (80ft 4⅛in), and height 5.65m (18ft 6½in).

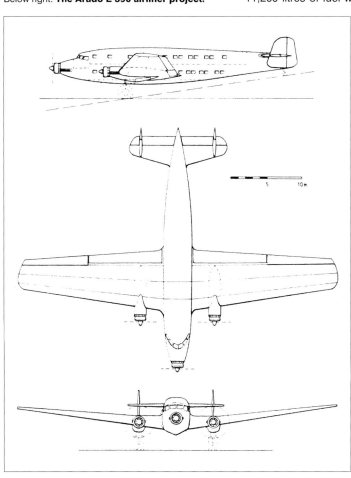

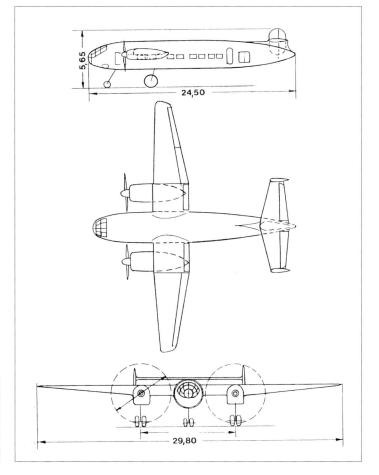

European Contest: Four-engined Foreign Competitors

We shall now cast a glance at design offices abroad, taking as examples those of France, the Netherlands, the USA and Great Britain, with the focus of attention on the latter.

In the British Isles the four-engined land-based transport appeared in the shape of the de Havilland DH 86 biplane, which, among others, was operated by Imperial Airways and British Airways. Possessing significantly more modern lines than the DH 86, which was based on the Dragon Rapide, was the elegant DH 91 Albatross – a particularly interesting aircraft that was almost entirely of wooden construction. With such aircraft, to which family the legendary DH 88 Comet racer belonged, de Havilland obtained important experience that was later to be used in the multi-purpose Mosquito. The Albatross took to its natural element for the

first time in May 1937, and the total of seven examples built were placed in service by Imperial Airways and by the RAF, although during the period 1941-43 all were lost in accidents.

In a different sphere the British were prominent with their long-range Empire flying boats built by Short Brothers. Names like Golden Hind and the Short-Mayo Composite with its Maia (lower) and Mercury (upper) components are recalled with joy by enthusiasts of this short epoch. However, in the sphere of large land-based civil transport aircraft, with the exception of one project Short had nothing spectacular to offer. This project, regrettably only taken as far as the partial realisation stage, consisted of a design bearing the designation S.32. Its specification dated from 1938, but due to the war, work on it was unfortunately terminated in May 1940. Documentary proof in the form of a photograph shows that it had advanced by March 1939 as far as fuselage construction.

The United States of America

Representative of the American aircraft industry are significant designs from the Douglas Aircraft Corporation, which were not only of high quality in pre-war years and entered airline service internationally in large numbers, but also epitomised the post-war picture in the aviation sphere. Together with Boeing and Lockheed, Douglas shared the largest slice of the market, and in terms of aircraft sold, the Europeans for many years were unable to stem the tide. It was only with the success of the Airbus that US manufacturers were presented with a serious contender, and the share of the 'cake' on the other side of the Atlantic became increasingly smaller.

However, back in the 'years of plenty', from its first one-off DC-1 commercial airliner, Douglas developed the improved DC-2, for which Fokker possessed the European sales rights. Compared to the rather clumsy-looking Junkers, the design of the Douglas aircraft, which entered regular service in May 1934, was more elegant from an aerodynamic aspect. From the DC-2 was developed the optimised DC-3 best-seller, flown for the first time in December 1935, which became *the* US airliner of the 1930s and 1940s. Both of these US types were extensively used in Europe, for example by KLM and Swissair, and were thus direct competitors to the rather conservatively conceived Ju 52.

Among the most important airliners of the post-war years, together with the successful Boeing and Lockheed models the DC-4 undoubtedly paved the way. Today, however, only a few examples are still in service as passenger transports. The history of this leading design goes back to the year 1935, when the

Technical Data for Various Dutch, Italian and French Aircraft

Manufacturer Type	Fokker F.XXXVI	Savoia-Marchetti SM 74	Dewoitine D.338
Powerplant	Wright Cyclone	Piaggio Stella X.RC	3 x Hispano-Suiza 9V 16/17
Take-off power, hp	750	700	650
Wingspan	33.00m (108' 3¼")	29.68m (97' 4½")	29.35m (96' 3½")
Length	23.60m (77' 5⅛")	21.36m (70' 1")	22.13m (72' 7¼")
Height	5.99m (18' 9⅞")	5.50m (18' 0½")	5.57m (18' 3¼")
Take-off weight, kg (lb)	16,500 (36,376)	14,000 (30,864)	11,150 (24,581)
Max speed, km/h (mph)	240 (149)	300 (186)	260 (162)
Range, km (miles)	1,350 (839)	1,000 (621)	1,950 (1,212)
Service ceiling, m (ft)	4,400 (14,435)	7,000 (22,965)	4,900 (10,800)
Passengers/crew	16-32/4	24-27/4	22/3
First flight	1934	1934	1935
Number built	62	3	31
Production period	1934/37	1934/35	1935/37

Technical Data for Various British Civil Aircraft

Manufacturer Type	de Havilland DH 86A	de Havilland DH 91	Armstrong-Whitworth AW 27 Ensign	Short Bros S.32
Powerplants	Gipsy Six I or II	Gipsy Twelve	AS Tiger IXC	Hercules VI C
Take-off power, hp	4 x 200/205*	4 x 525	4 x 850	4 x 1,650
Wingspan	19.66m (64' 6")	31.90m (104' 8")	37.49m (123' 0")	38.86m (127' 6")
Length	14.05m (46' 1")	21.33m (70' 0")	33.83m (111' 0")	27.66m (90' 9")
Height	3.96m (13' 0")	6.15m (20' 2")	7.01m (23' 0")	-
Wing area, m² (ft²)	59.55 (641)	100.16 (1,078)	227.62 (2,450)	187.67 (2,020)
Empty weight, kg (lb)	3,218* (7,228)	9,207* (20,298)	14,932 (32,920)	17,713 (39,050)
Take-off weight, kg (lb)	4,990* (11,000)	13,381* (29,500)	22,000 (48,500)	32,205 (71,000)
Max speed, km/h (mph)	241* (150)	362* (225)	322 (200) at 2,200m (7,200ft)	531* (330)
Cruising speed, km/h (mph)	217* (135)	-	274 (200)	-
Range, km (miles)	1,204* (748)	1,674* (1,040)	1,384 (860)	5,472 (3,400)
Service ceiling, m (ft)	5,486* (18,000)	5,456* (17,900)	6,705 (22,000)	7,620* (25,000)
Passengers/Crew	10/1-2	22/4*	27-40/5	12-24/5-7
Production period	1933/37	1937/39	1938/40	1939/40
Numbers built	62	7	14	(3 fuselages)
First flight date	14.01.1934	20.05.1937	23.01.1938	none

* Figures relate to Gipsy Six II engine installation (DH 86); to the passenger version (DH 91); and to speed at pressure-cabin altitude (Short S.32)

The Douglas-developed DC-4E, over-dimensioned and far ahead of its time.

The DC-4E prototype accomplished its maiden flight on 7th June 1938.

DC-4E project originated. As the development of air travel had shown at the time, it was very ambitious. Among the Douglas commercial airliners, the DC-4E was its first four-engined development. In that year five notable airlines – Pan Am, TWA, United, Eastern, and American Airlines – drew up the requirements for an airliner intended for use over long distances and capable of carrying a maximum of 50 passengers. In order to operate at high altitudes while transporting the passenger in comfort, the requirements included a pressurised cabin. Development costs of this early 'Jumbo' were met by Douglas and the other airlines named, except for Pan Am and TWA, which, despite their initial interest, turned to the Boeing 307 project.

The development and manufacture of the DC-4E prototype was completed in the space of just two years, and in May 1938 an aircraft that exceeded all previous standards was rolled out of the final assembly hall. In contrast to the Boeing Stratoliner, and the Focke-Wulf Condor and Junkers Ju 90, which made the headlines on the other side of the Atlantic, the DC-4E was designed to incorporate a tricycle nosewheel undercarriage, providing the pilot with optimal vision and handling qualities. Its roomy fuselage had a length of 29.74m (97ft 7in) and allowed comfortable seating for up to 52 passengers. The empennage had triple fins and rudders, comparable with future designs such as the Lockheed Constellation or the Avro York. The low-positioned wing design strongly resembled that of the DC-3 and had a span of 42.14m (138ft 3in) and a wing area of 200.21m² (2,155ft²), the trailing-edge having split- and slotted flaps. Power was provided by four Pratt

& Whitney R-2180 Twin Hornet 14-cylinder twin-row radials of 35.72 litres cubic capacity (2,180in³), delivering a maximum of 1,450hp from three-bladed Hamilton-Standard variable-pitch metal airscrews. A total of 8,327 litres of fuel was carried in the wing tanks.

Following its roll-out in May 1938, the first flight was planned for 7th June, when pilots Carl Cover and John Cable lifted the Douglas 'Jumbo' off on its 90-minute flight. Its route led from the works airfield to Mines Field and the impressions gained of its handling characteristics and other criteria were initially optimistic. Further test flights were conducted on the following day with a strengthened crew complement, and upon the conclusion of the flight trials Douglas received the DC-4E'a all-important airworthiness certificate. In the following year, United Airlines took over the aircraft and conducted a further series of tests with it. Designated the Super Mainliner, the aircraft performed a series of demonstration flights all over

the USA. The public relations machine was in full swing, during which pilot Benny Howard caused considerable excitement with a spectacular two-engined take-off from Cheyenne Airport in Wyoming. Unfortunately, during the course of its 500-hour airline testing programme, some serious deficiencies came to light with regard to its anticipated performance parameters. Its 3.5-ton overweight reduced its range and speed and, not least, its profitability. A further reason for the failure of the DC-4E was undoubtedly its enormous size. The decisive factor, however, was probably the unpredictable political situation at that time, which made long-term planning by the airlines extremely difficult. Following the rejection of the DC-4E, from 1939 Douglas worked on a more contemporary concept – the later very successful DC-4 – and the sole DC-4E was sold to Japan Airlines after export approval had been granted. With Nippon, however, the aircraft was to be put to a very different use from

The DC-4 corresponded to the existing circumstances of the time, but was initially produced as the C-54 military transport. In the post-war period, Douglas was able to make an international breakthrough with the commercial DC-4.

A leased DC-4 freighter in the colours of the new Lufthansa.

TWA and Pan Am provided the impulse for the Boeing 307, an aircraft that incorporated several components of the B-17 bomber in its design.

that anticipated: it was to serve as the basis for a long-range bomber project for the Imperial Japanese Navy. Its purchase by the airline was simply a clever diversionary manoeuvre, and soon afterwards the deliberately false report was circulated that the DC-4E had crashed in Tokyo Bay. In fact it had been transferred under the greatest secrecy to Nakajima, where the former Mainliner became the object of study for the bomber programme, since little experience had been available in Japan with aircraft of its size. Manufacture of the Nakajima G5NI Shin-zan (Mountain recess) four-engined bomber prototype was completed by around March 1941, but mediocre performance of this Japanese product also ended in termination of the project after only a few prototypes had been built.

Meanwhile, the timely solution for a modern commercial aircraft was established by Douglas, together with the airlines, and summarised in a catalogue of requirements. Although these resulted in a new design, it incorporated the knowledge gained with the DC-4E. The completely new DC-4 project was now pursued by its former design team led by designers A E Raymond and E F Burton. This more modest solution consisted of an aircraft accommodating a maximum of 42 seated passengers or 28 in a 'sleeper' configuration. The DC-4's suitability for intercontinental flights was also stressed, and its technical modifications over the DC-4E were considerable. It had a shorter fuselage, centrally mounted fin and rudder, twin undercarriage mainwheels, and the use of a pressurised cabin was dispensed with. For motive power, two makes of engine were available: the Wright Cyclone and the Pratt & Whitney R-2000 Twin Wasp; the latter was used in all American series-produced versions of the DC-4, as well as in the Skymaster. The design featured rubber de-icing strips in all the usual positions, while the smaller airframe dimensions enabled a lower constructional weight that reduced the take-off weight by some 7,000kg (15,432 lb), less than that of the DC-4E. The suitability of this 'streamlined' design proved convincing to American, Eastern, and United Airlines, but in the years to come the future of the DC-4 turned out to be quite other than anticipated. The Japanese attack on the American Fleet's base at Pearl Harbor on 7th

The beginnings of the later very successful Constellation series. Initially placed in service by the USAAF in limited numbers as the C-69, its heyday began in a completely different epoch in which only photographs and recollections of the Ju 90 remained.

Between these two photographs there is a world of difference. The Dutch Fokker F.XXXVI flew for the first time in 1934 and represents the technology of the early 1930s.

Technical Data for Various US Aircraft

| Manufacturer | Douglas | Douglas | Boeing | Boeing |
Type	DC-4E	DC-4-1009	307 Stratoliner	B-377 Stratocruiser
Powerplants (4)	Pratt & Whitney R-2180-S1A1G	Pratt & Whitney R-2000-9	Wright GR-1820	Pratt & Whitney R-4360
Take-off power, hp	1,450	1,450	1,200	3,500
Fuel capacity, litres (US gals)	8,327 (2,196)	10,866* (2,868)	8,600 (2,270)	29,500 (7,786)
Wingspan	42.14m (138' 3")	35.81m (117' 6")	32.69m (107' 3")	43.05m (141' 3")
Length	29.74m (97' 7")	28.60m (93' 10")	22.67m (74' 5")	33.63m (110' 4")
Height	7.48m (24' 6")	8.38m (27' 6")	6.33m (20' 9")	11.66m (38' 3")
Wing area, m² (ft²)	200.21 (2,155)	135.63 (1,460)	138.05 (1,486)	164.20 (1,767)
Empty weight, kg (lb)	19,308 (42,570)	19,641 (43,300)	13,730 (30,270)	35,751 (78,820)
Take-off weight, kg (lb)	30,164 (66,500)	33,1l3 (73,000)	20,385 (44,940)	66,680 (147,000)
Wing loading, kg/m² (lb/ft²)	139.3 (30.86)	212.4 (43.50)	147.7 (30.24)	406.1 (83.20)
Max speed, km/h (mph)	394 (245)	451 (280)	396 (246)	605 (376)
Cruising speed, km/h (mph)	322 (200)	365 (227)	354 (220)	505 (314)
Range (normal), km (miles)	3,540 (2,200)	3,600 (2,240)	3,050 (1,900)	5,500 (3,420)
Range (max), km (miles)	-	4,700 (2,920)	3,864 (2,400)	7,360 (4,570)
Service ceiling, m (ft)	6,980 (22,900)	6,800 (22,300)	8,000 (26,250)	10,500 (34,450)

* Maximum fuel 13,596 litres (3,592 US gallons)

December 1941 meant that the United States was now officially drawn into the war. The dreaded military confrontation with Imperial Japan had now become reality. Besides a host of military machines, the US armed forces now needed a fleet of transport aircraft to overcome the not inconsiderable logistics problems. From now on, the formerly civilian-use project was pursued strictly with military ends in mind, and instead of airline logos, the first 24 aircraft, originally intended for the previously mentioned airlines, now sported the much less appealing olive-green 'uniform'.

In its new configuration the DC-4 was designated the C-54 Skymaster. The first example made its maiden flight on 14th February 1942, and entered military service on 20th March. All other versions that made their appearance, continually optimised to meet military needs during the war, were taken over by the USAAF. The extremely effective Skymaster formed the backbone of the transport squadrons of both the Army Air Force and the US Navy. The concluding version of this successful development series was the C-54G.

Some months before the collapse of Imperial Japan a significant number of aircraft on order were cancelled by the procurement authorities that affected all the US aircraft manufacturers. After the last large-scale orders had left the final assembly lines in 1945, production soon settled down to a peacetime pace. Douglas was no exception, for already during the war the company had been considering a successful marketing campaign for its DC-4 airliner, once freed from its imposed military 'uniform', and the time soon arrived to consider the rebirth of civil transport after the collapse of the Axis Powers. In this respect, those in responsible positions in the airlines, the aircraft firms and, not least, the politicians had to make their contributions.

In the autumn of 1945 Douglas began production of the DC-4-1009, the first example, c/n 42904, was delivered to Western Airlines, registered NC 10201. With the exception of internal fittings, the design features of the DC-4-1009 displayed no serious alterations compared to the Skymaster. In its initial configuration, the DC-4 airliner was able to carry 44 passengers, and in the so-called 'sleeper' version could accommodate 28. In airline service, its passenger capacity often varied considerably. From 1953 Swissair increased the capacity to 55 passengers, but that was still by no means enough. On various airlines, seating was raised to a so-called 'high-density' level to almost double that originally intended; as a rule the accommodation possibilities varied from 62 or 74 to a maximum of 86 seats. Besides the DC-4-1009, these modifications were also applied to several Skymasters that had been turned to civil use. As in the case of the C-54, Douglas also dispensed with a pressurised cabin for the DC-4-1009. From a purely constructional aspect, equipping the aircraft with pressurised air was certainly possible, but the airlines concerned made no use of this possibility.

Douglas was nevertheless able to secure a large portion of the market that had been fought for with 'clenched fists', since thus far the cake had been portioned out without the Europeans. However, with the appearance of Airbus Industries the situation drastically changed for the hitherto all-powerful US aircraft. Over the years Douglas consistently pursued development of its commercial airliner series, which materialised in the shape of the DC-8 and DC-9 as well as numerous subsequent models. The 'wide-body' DC-10 and its follow-on, the MD-11, made the leap into a completely different dimension.

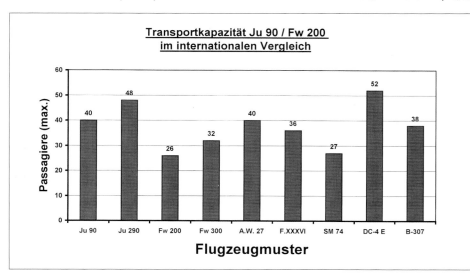

Passenger capacities of various nationalities of airliners compared.

Chapter Five

The Ju 90 in Series Production

Werknummern 900001 to 900010

As mentioned previously, the V4 prototype served as a basis for the series production models under the designations Ju 90Z-2 and Z-3. The three aircraft ordered by Lufthansa in November 1938 consisted of Werknummern 4916, 900001 and 900003. These were followed by a further order for two aircraft, 900006 and 900007. As a successor to the V2 that was lost at Bathurst, DLH introduced 900005 into service, christening it the *Preussen* like its forbear. In addition to the orders from DLH, there were two others ordered from abroad, by SAA, which already possessed the Ju 86. Due to the outbreak of war, the insurmountable barrier between Germany and South Africa, a Commonwealth country, prevented the aircraft from being delivered and resulted in them being taken over by the RLM; the two aircraft concerned were the Ju 90Z-3s with Werknummern 900002 and 900006, which were to have been powered by the Pratt & Whitney Twin Wasp, all others having the BMW 132 from the very outset. The most important data for each of these aircraft is provided in the table overleaf.

Top: **The Ju 90 V1** *Der Große Dessauer* **pictured during one of its many test flights.**

Right: **The Ju 90 V1 fuselage structure during application of the sheet skinning.**

Far right: **An internal view of the Ju 90 V1 fuselage, showing the longerons and transverse frames.**

Data for Ju 90s Werknummern 900001 to 900010

Version	Werk-Nr	First Flight	Civil Reg	Luftwaffe Reg	Remarks
Z-2	900001	24.02.1939	D-ABDG	GF+GB	*Württemberg*. Operated by DLH, then became V12, and again used by DLH. Captured by British troops in Travemünde in May 1945
Z-3	900002	21.07.1939	D-APZR	KB+LA, J4 +EH	Originally ZS-ANG for SAA but not delivered. Used initially by GLF, then to Junkers. Accident in Leipheim with Me 321. Destroyed in crash near Bad Tölz 11.09.1943
Z-2	900003	10.03.1939	D-ADFJ	GF+GA, J4+FH	Initially used by DLH, then LVG Berlin. Later took part in Iraq operation. Destroyed by bombs in Italy 20.05.1943. Christened *Baden* by DLH
Z-3	900004	02.11.1939	ZS-ANH	KB+LB	SAA registration, but not delivered. Used by GLF. Burned out in take-off accident in Hamburg 12.04.1940.
Z-2	900005	03.04.1939	D-AEDS	GF+GE, J4+GH	*Preussen*. Initially to DLH, then to LVG Berlin and back to DLH. Took part in Iraq operation as G6+CY as Luftwaffe transport. Captured by British troops May 1945
Z-2	900006	14.06.1939	D-ASND	BX+GX, J4+HH	Used by DLH and LVG Berlin. Destroyed during transport mission 1943. *Mecklenburg*
Z-2	900007	19.10.1939	D-AFHG	BG+GY, J4+JH	*Oldenburg*. Used by DLH, then LVG Berlin. Made emergency ditching when shot down near Corsica 23.07.1944.
Z-2	900008	04.02.1940	D-ATDC	BG+GZ	*Hessen*. Used by DLH, then LVG. Damaged in transport op, and blown up near Kharkov in January 1943
Z-2	900009	06.03.1940	D-AJHB	BJ+OV, J4+KH	*Thüringen*. Used by DLH, then LVG. Used in Iraq operation. Later modified as experimental aircraft in Travemünde (E-Stelle Tarnewitz) where it was destroyed in August 1944
Z-2	900010	25.04.1940	D-AVMF	-	*Brandenburg*. Used by DLH. Destroyed 08.11.1940 in crash due to icing-up

Key: DLH Deutsche Lufthansa; GLF Generalluftzeugmeister Flugbereitschaft (GL Air-Readiness Unit); LVG Luftverkehrsgruppe (Air Transport Group) Berlin; SAA South African Airways

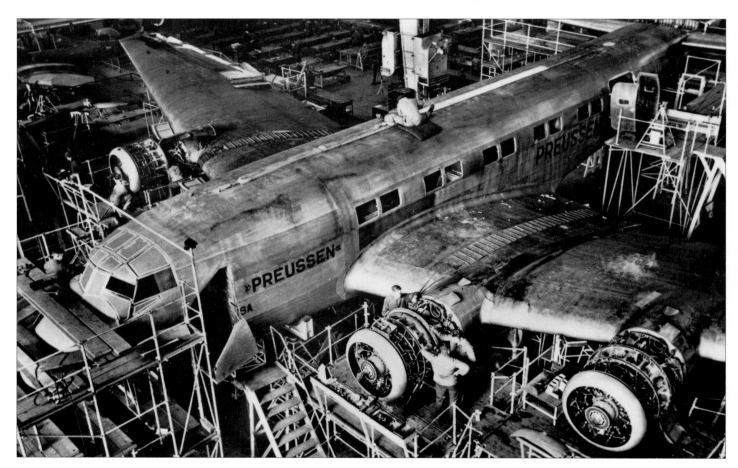

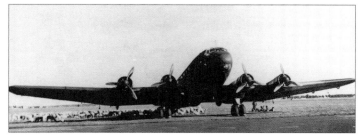

Chapter Six

The Technical Design of the Ju 90Z-2

We shall now take a look at the technical design of the Ju 90, which was undoubtedly drawn up in accordance with the latest technical knowledge of the time. It clearly illustrates the diversion from the certainly extremely robust but, from the aerodynamic point of view, long outmoded corrugated sheet-skinning type of construction that had already been dispensed with on the Ju 86, Ju 160, and on the military Ju 89. Only in the empennage area of the Ju 90 was the traditional Junkers method of construction retained.

Returning now to Dipl.-Ing. Ernst Zindel, the 'father' of the Ju 90, he compared several of its features with the earlier Ju 52: 'A comparative picture of the increase in size and volume between the Ju 52 and the Ju 90 is presented by the following figures [see table below]. It is clear from the figures that the Ju 90's increase in engine power, at 3,360hp, is 1.68 times that of the 2,000hp for the Ju 52. For the Ju 90, this gives:

- an increase in payload by a factor of 2.35
- 3.5 times the volume of passenger space
- 2.5 times the number of passengers
- 4 times the freight space

'With a simultaneous increase of 50% in normal range and 65km/h (40mph) in speed. By increasing the engine power to 5,600hp, which corresponds roughly to the available increase in payload capacity, the cruising speed is raised from 250km/h (155mph) to 400km/h (249mph), that is by no less than 150km/h (93mph).

'This increase in specific performance with the Ju 90 was only possible through a significant aerodynamic improvement of the entire aircraft as well as the associated overall general development of the entire design.'

Photographs on the opposite page:

Top: **The first *Preussen* for DLH in an advanced stage of the construction process.**

Bottom left: **The Ju 90 V4 *Schwabenland*, later *Sachsen*, seen with Luftwaffe call-sign KH+XA.**

Bottom right: **The Ju 90 V5. With this aircraft the next stage of development began – with the Ju 290.**

The Reason for Four Engines

Zindel continues: 'The first, very simple reason for the choice of four engines in the Ju 90 is that at the time of the Ju 90's development, no engines of sufficient power were available that, with only three, would have provided the necessary power for an aircraft of this size, which, for the abovementioned reasons, we had deemed necessary.

'The second reason, very often cited as the chief advantage of the four-motor arrangement over the three-motor one, is that by dispensing with the central engine, visibility for the pilot as well as the noise level in the passenger cabin is considerably improved. However, this appears to us less decisive; rather, we are of the view that by taking suitable measures, these improvements can also be achieved in sufficient measure with the three-motor layout.

'As with all other Junkers transport aircraft, the Ju 90 is a cantilever low-wing monoplane of all-metal construction. The main construction material is Duralumin, the proven German light-metal material that with special techniques – Plattierung und Eloxierung [anodic treatment] – possesses first-rate corrosion resistance. A considerable volume of Electron metal is also employed in the form of cast and moulded parts, and for particularly highly-stressed components, high-grade steel is used. Wings and tail surfaces are multi-sparred, covered with a load-bearing skin. By using large, easily remov-able skin panels that can be quickly and securely screwed, an extraordinarily high accessibility, and hence simple and secure control and maintenance of all internal compartments of the wing and tail surfaces as also all steering and regulatory components, can be achieved. The fuselage consists of a simple and clearly arranged stiff shell. As with all modern fast transport aircraft, the undercarriage is hydraulically retractable and is completely enclosed behind the engine nacelles, the tail-wheel being likewise retracted into the fuselage.

'The entire airframe, all control and servicing components as well as the entire powerplant system have been designed to be very robust and reliable, based on a thousandfold proven experience in air travel. It can thus certainly be taken for granted that in practical use the Ju 90 will display equally good if not better qualities in terms of reliability, lower maintenance and support costs and longer operating times between individual overhaul periods than, in this respect, the already proven and particularly economic Ju 52.

'From the very beginning, the design was laid out in close co-operation with the development and manufacturing workshops to possess the utmost simplicity and economy of manufacture, which itself reflects significantly on the production costs of the aircraft. A noteworthy feature is that despite its size, through a suitable breakdown of the component parts, it is possible to load it on a rail freight car.

Comparison of the Ju 52 and Ju 90

Aircraft	Ju 90	Ju 52
Wingspan	35m (114' 10")	29m (95' 1.7")
Wing area, m² (ft²)	184 (1,980.5)	110 (1,184.0)
Fuselage width	3.00m (9' 10⅛")	1.75m (5' 8⅞")
Passengers, normal	38-40	15-17
Floor area, passenger (cabin and related rooms), m² (ft²)	37 (398.26)	10 (107.64)
Usable volume of passenger cabins, m³ (ft³)	75 (2,648.5)	21 (741.58)
Volume, freight compartments, m³ (ft³)	25 (882.83)	6 (211.88)
Payload with fully-occupied cabin, including baggage and freight, kg (lb)	4,000-6,000 (8,818-13,228)	1,700 (3,748)
Normal range, km (miles)	1,500 (932)	1,000 (621)
Cruising speed at normal range, km/h (mph)	325-400 (202-249)	250-280 (155-174)

Note: With a corresponding reduction in the volume of payload, the range of the Ju 90 could be increased without any problem to 3,000-4,000km (1,864-2,486 miles).

'Deviating from all previous Junkers aircraft well known to have been of corrugated sheet-metal skinning up to the Ju 52, on the Ju 90 the entire skinning is of flat sheeting. This measure was necessary to reduce the detrimental drag of the aircraft, since with an aircraft of its size and with relatively small engine power, the good flying performance and high transportation achieved could only be attained through careful aerodynamic configuration and optimal design of the entire airframe. This will become clear when I tell you that the overall drag of the Ju 90 at the same airspeed is no greater than that of the Ju 52.

'For shortening the take-off and landing run, the aircraft is equipped with flaps that, like the elevators and the undercarriage, are hydraulically operated.'

So much for the extremely useful commentary from designer Ernst Zindel. In order to provide as exact and comprehensive a portrayal as possible of this technologically advanced aircraft, we shall now enter the technical realm of this Junkers 'giant'. The following technical details are based on original documents, and are given in their original form with corresponding illustrations from the handbook. I have consciously avoided personal comment so that the historical material can maintain its absolute authenticity. Lack of space means that only extracts are possible, so I have concentrated on the more significant details. The reader will find descriptions of the individual components based chiefly on original documents, and only where there is a lack of historical material has recourse been made to reliable secondary literature, as listed at the end of the book.

Data on other Ju 90 production series is included where relevant.

The Fuselage

The Ju 90 fuselage was of the semi-monocoque type of construction, as was the norm at that time, and covered with smooth sheet-metal skinning. Behind the cockpit came the radio compartment, followed by the galley and cloakroom or storage area. The passenger area, designed to accommodate 40 passengers, was divided into five separate compartments: sections I and II were reserved for smokers, the remaining three for non-smokers. Towards the fuselage rear were located two washrooms and a cloakroom. In the course of series production, the rectangular passenger windows were situated at various locations, while in the V5, V6, V7 and V8 prototypes they took the form of much smaller porthole-type windows. At the rearmost end of the usable space was a storage room for mail or luggage. In the case of the V1 to V6 prototypes, the overall length of the fuselage was 26.45m (86ft 9⅜in), and in the V7 and V8 28.50m (96ft 6in), of which the passenger area had a length of 10.20m (33ft 5½in), with a fuselage width of 2.85m (9ft 4¼in).

The Ju 90 handbook has this to say on the subject: The fuselage is constructed as a shell, strengthened with continuous longerons and vertically arranged frames. Attached to the one-piece fuselage at its forward extremity is the fuselage nose, fabricated of wood and fastened with screw-bolts, the rear end structure being connected with detachable thrust nipple strips. Since the entire fuselage longitudinal sections ahead of frames 7 and 12 are slotted together, the fuselage can be separated at these points for repair or alteration.

The fuselage is firmly attached to the wing centre section, which is fastened to it by 12 screw-bolts. The variable elevator surfaces are attached to the rear fuselage at frame 19 by two forked anchorings. In a channel running along the centre of the fuselage, which continues at a right angle into the wings, are housed the push-

The fuselage nose housed the fresh-air intake and the landing lights.

The sheet-metal panels were accurately placed before riveting.

pull control rods, engine connecting rods, etc.

The fuselage is divided into the cockpit, the forward usable space with parlour, the passenger cabin, the rear usable space with toilets, the trim loading room and the traversable rear end of the fuselage.

Cockpit Details

The very spaciously arranged cockpit area was the aircraft's 'nerve centre', and was fitted out with the most modern equipment of the time. In shape and size, it was certainly generously dimensioned; however, the 'trimmings', in terms of an ergonomic arrangement, were not yet a main priority.

On this subject, Ernst Zindel remarked: 'The extremely spacious and purpose-designed cockpit – the "eye" and "brain" of the aircraft – offers the three-man flight crew the best working conditions, and visibility for both pilots is particularly favourable. Dual controls, blind-flying instruments, reflection-free nocturnal lighting, blind-landing instrumentation and direction-finding equipment, as well as various items of navigational equipment, are of course available. Course steering and the possibility of autopilot installation are catered for. In the cockpit, shortwave and long-wave main stations are likewise installed. The best working conditions for the individual crew members thus guarantee excellent co-operation of the entire crew of the aircraft.'

The Handbook contains the following description: The cockpit for the three-man crew is completely enclosed and covered over. The seats for the two pilots are identically arranged on each side of the aircraft centreline. At right-angles to the direction of flight is the radio operator's seat between fuselage frames 2 and 3.

Access to the cockpit is via a ramp situated on the fuselage port side through which the forward baggage compartment can also be loaded. The fuselage nose is accessible from a swivel door situated beneath.

At the centre of frame 3 is a connecting swing door from the cockpit, with a built-in Plexiglas window, which leads to the forward usable space. To the right of this, behind the cockpit, is the swing door to the baggage room.

To enable easier supervision of the shafts and equipment housed beneath the cockpit flooring, the latter consists largely of removable access hatches. Access to the conduits in the control channels is by removable side-opening hatches. In the cockpit upper decking is a sliding window that can be opened towards the rear by a handgrip and can be used as an emergency exit by the crew. Plexiglas is used for the windows, with the exception of the four forward clear-vision panels of Verbundglas [laminated glass] and the side window opening, made of Sekurit. For protection against the sun, the cockpit dorsal and side window panels can be covered with green sliding curtains.

A view from inside the enormous fuselage, looking towards the cockpit.

Plan and side views of the Ju 90 with principal dimensions (Handbook, Part T.A.).

Details of the numbered wing and fuselage frames and spars (Handbook, Part T.A.).

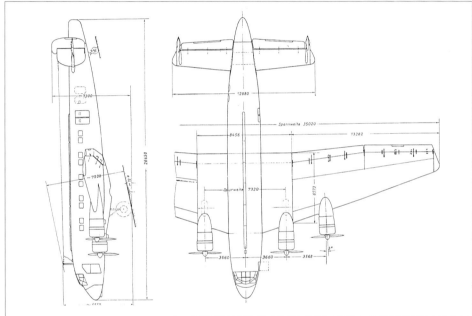

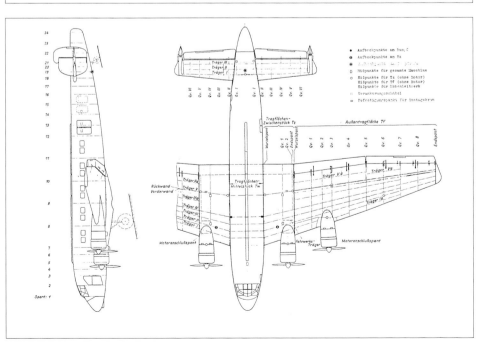

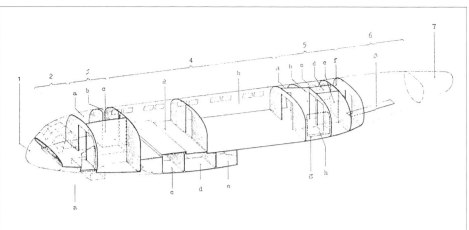

Section 1: Fuselage nose

Section 2: Cockpit
a) Loading ramp

Section 3: Forward usable space
a) Galley
b) Cloakroom
c) Large baggage room

Section 4: Passenger cabins
a) Smokers' area
b) Non-smokers' area
c,d,e) Loading bays

Section 5: Rear usable space
a) Toilet
b) Vestibule
c) Mail room

d) Cloakroom
e) Toilet
f) Trim-load room
g) Door
h) Baggage room

Section 6: Rear fuselage
a) Gangway

Section 7: Fuselage tailcone

To enable observation of the landing area being approached, the radio operator has a square Plexiglas window situated at a suitable height between frames 1 and 2 and between frames 3 and 4.

All the radio equipment, with the exception of the antenna portion, is located in the cockpit on the right wall of the fuselage between frames 2 and 3 and on the front face of frame 3. Also located there are the switchboard and distributor panels for the electrical installations.

Forward Usable Space

The forward usable space situated behind the cockpit between frames 3 and 7 consists of the large baggage room of 6.7m³ (236.6ft³) volume, which is loaded via the forward sliding ramp and cockpit. The remaining space forward serves as a galley and simultaneously as the corridor between the cockpit and the passenger cabin. The latter third of the corridor serves as the cloakroom for some of the passengers. In this area, in the middle of frame 7, is located a swivel door to the passenger cabin.

Passenger Cabin

The passenger cabin extends from frames 7 to 12 and is divided into smoking and non-smoking compartments. The two sections are divided at frame 9 by a fixed partition wall. Access from the vestibule to the passenger cabin is via sliding doors located at the centre of frame 12. At the left and right side walls of the fuselage are ten windows arranged in pairs of five on each side. All of the Plexiglas windows serve as emergency exits and can be easily withdrawn inwards by a hand lever located at the top of each. Beneath the passenger cabins are three luggage compartments between supporting beam 2 and frame 10. These compartments have a total volume of 10m³ (35.3ft³); loading takes place through four twin-door hatches in the fuselage underside.

Ernst Zindel remarked in this connection: 'In the Ju 90 particular value was placed on the comfortable, functional and favourable interior arrangements of the passenger compartments. As already mentioned, the layout caters for a maximum of 40 passengers. According to requirements, or at the special wish of the owner, various internal layouts and decors are possible. Normal outfitting, as you can see in the presentation aircraft, shows five completely separate compartments, each with comfortable upholstered seats facing each other, similar to that in a railway compartment or dining-car. As in a dining-car, tables are arranged between the seats. Alternative arrangements are:

- Seats facing each other in the forward cabin
- Seats one behind the other in the rear cabin
- Complete or partial arrangements with reclining armchairs, especially for long distances and night flights

Opposite page:

Top: **Space sub-divisions in the Ju 90 fuselage (Handbook, Part 1).**

Bottom: **The use of a tailwheel meant that the crew's optimum visibility was reduced.**

This page:

Right: **The two halves of the cockpit with 'stand-ins' posing as crew members.**

Below: **The view inside the roomy cockpit with its extensively glazed vision panels.**

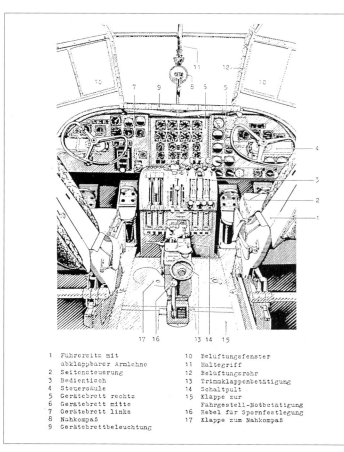

1	Führersitz mit abklappbarer Armlehne	10	Belüftungsfenster
2	Seitensteuerung	11	Haltegriff
3	Bedientisch	12	Belüftungsrohr
4	Steuersäule	13	Trimmklappenbetätigung
5	Gerätebrett rechts	14	Schaltpult
6	Gerätebrett mitte	15	Klappe zur Fahrgestell-Notbetätigung
7	Gerätebrett links	16	Hebel für Spornfestlegung
8	Nahkompaß	17	Klappe zum Nahkompaß
9	Gerätebrettbeleuchtung		

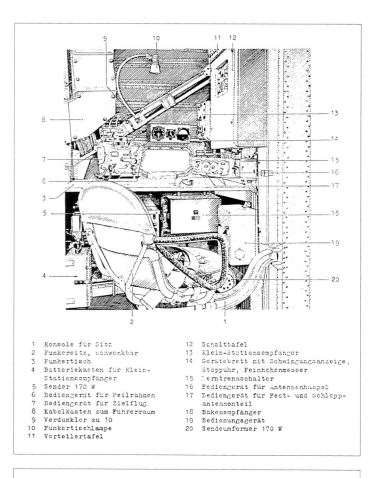

1	Konsole für Sitz	12	Schalttafel
2	Funkersitz, schwenkbar	13	Klein-Stationsempfänger
3	Funkertisch	14	Gerätebrett mit Schwingungsanzeige, Stoppuhr, Feinhöhenmesser
4	Batteriekasten für Klein-Stationsempfänger	15	F-erntrennschalter
5	Sender 170 W	16	Bediengerät für Antennenhaspel
6	Bediengerät für Peilrahmen	17	Bediengerät für Fest- und Schlepp-antennenteil
7	Bediengerät für Zielflug	18	Bakenempfänger
8	Kabelkasten zum Führerraum	19	Bedienungsgerät
9	Verdunkler zu 10	20	Sendeumformer 170 W
10	Funkertischlampe		
11	Verteilertafel		

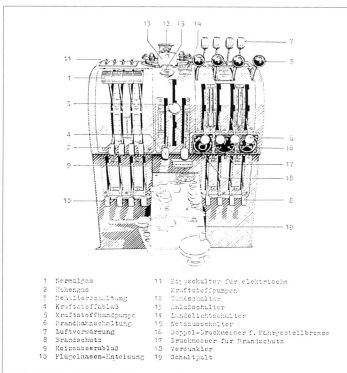

1	Normalgas	11	Kippschalter für elektrische Kraftstoffpumpen
2	Höhengas	12	Zundschalter
3	Behälterschaltung	13	Anlaßschalter
4	Kraftstoffablaß	14	Landelichtschalter
5	Kraftstoffhandpumpe	15	Netzausschalter
6	Brandhahnschaltung	16	Doppel-Druckmesser f. Fahrgestellbremse
7	Luftvorwärmung	17	Druckmesser für Brandschutz
8	Brandschutz	18	Verdunkler
9	Heizwasserablaß	19	Schaltpult
10	Flügelnasen-Enteisung		

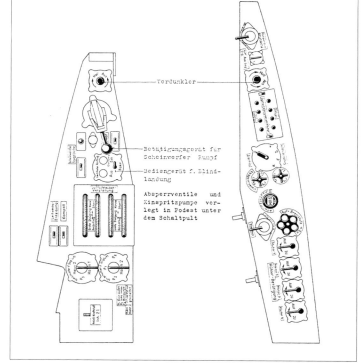

Illustrations on this page:

Top left: **Cockpit arrangement in the Ju 90 V4 (Handbook, Part 1).**

Top right: **The radio operator's position (Handbook, Part 1).**

Bottom left: **Close-up of the central control console (Handbook, Part 7).**

Bottom right: **Left and right dashboards in the cockpit (Handbook, Part 7).**

Opposite page, clockwise from top left:

This compartment displays a cosy atmosphere.
The view inside the non-smoking cabin.
Air hostesses attended to physical needs.
Whoever could afford this type of travel, could well laugh!
Two washrooms/toilets were located behind the non-smoking cabin.
The internal furnishings in the Ju 90 varied.

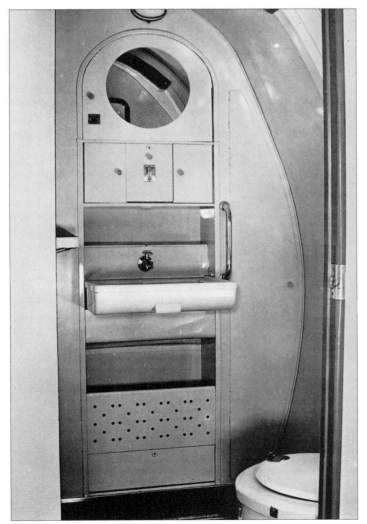

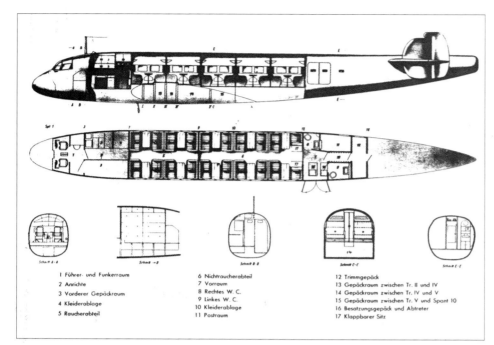

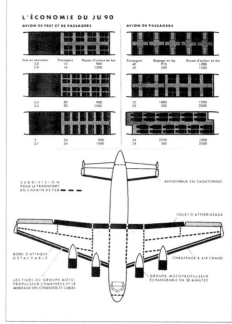

1 Führer- und Funkerraum
2 Anrichte
3 Vorderer Gepäckraum
4 Kleiderablage
5 Raucherabteil
6 Nichtraucherabteil
7 Vorraum
8 Rechtes W. C.
9 Linkes W. C.
10 Kleiderablage
11 Postraum
12 Trimmgepäck
13 Gepäckraum zwischen Tr. II und IV
14 Gepäckraum zwischen Tr. IV und V
15 Gepäckraum zwischen Tr. V und Spant 10
16 Besatzungsgepäck und Abtreter
17 Klappbarer Sitz

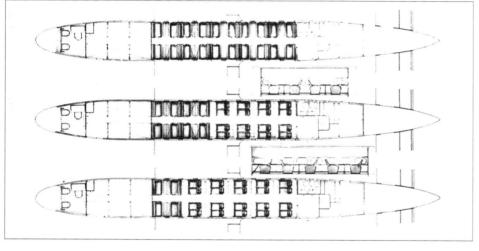

Top left: **Space arrangement in the Ju 90.**

Above: **A French journal published various planned seating schemes for the Ju 90.**

Centre: **Three different cabin arrangements for 40, 32 and 28 passengers (Ju 90 V9).**

Bottom: **This illustration of a 'private air-yacht' was published in 1938 in *Schweizer Illustrierte Zeitung* (Swiss Illustrated Newspaper).**

'The very effective air-circulation system with an envisaged air exchange volume of 600-800 litres per passenger per minute, as well as an additional fresh-air 'shower' for each passenger, ensures superb air circulation, one of the most important requisites for a pleasant and cosy sojourn in an aircraft. In the same manner, at low outside temperatures, a heating system using heat from the engine exhaust gases, maintains the cabin air temperature at a comfortable level.

'Particular care has been taken in the Ju 90 to maintain low-noise insulation and sound-proofing in the passenger cabins. The formerly very often uncomfortable exhaust emissions and noise from the engines, propellers and so on, find their way into the cabins by every means imaginable, be it through slits and cracks, and especially via the air circulation openings and so forth. By the employment of effective systematic insulation, sound-proofing and noise isolation – via all the paths through which noise is normally transmitted through the structure and air channels – it has become possible to reduce these noise level in the Ju 90 to one not yet attained in most means of transportation. Measurements with the Ju 90 have revealed that the noise level in the passenger cabin is less than that in a railway carriage, so that conversation at normal speech level is easily possible; thus one of the most noticeable previous deficiencies in an aircraft has been eliminated.'

'The architectural arrangement of the passenger cabins was developed in co-operation with the well-known architect Prof. Breuhaus of DLH, involving comfortable seats for the passengers, tasteful furnishings for the armchairs, walls and ceiling decors, diffused ceiling lighting and individual reading lamps for the passengers, an electrical summoning system for the steward and the like – all measures for the comfort and well-being of the passengers. The seating comfort, the tasteful and practical furnishings and the completely new spaciousness of a passenger cabin the size of the Ju 90 are best gained from a personal inspection.

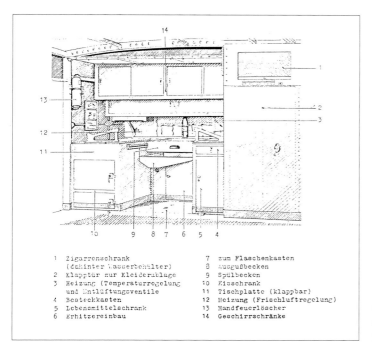

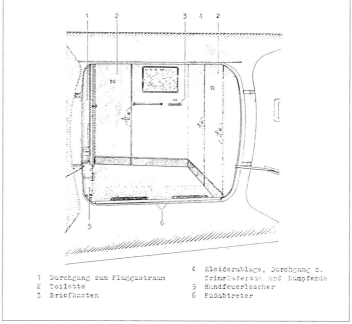

1 Zigarrenschrank (dahinter Wasserbehälter)	7 zum Flaschenkasten
2 Klapptür zur Kleiderablage	8 Ausgußbecken
3 Heizung (Temperaturregelung und Entlüftungsventile)	9 Spülbecken
4 Besteckkasten	10 Eisschrank
5 Lebensmittelschrank	11 Tischplatte (klappbar)
6 Erhitzereinbau	12 Heizung (Frischluftregelung)
	13 Handfeuerlöscher
	14 Geschirrschränke

1 Durchgang zum Fluggastraum	4 Kleiderablage, Durchgang z. Trimmladeraum u. Rumpfende
2 Toilette	5 Handfeuerlöscher
3 Briefkasten	6 Fußabtreter

Rear Usable Space

Regarding the rear usable space behind the passenger cabins, the Handbook has this to say: The rear usable space is connected to the passenger cabin and consists of the vestibule, two toilets and a cloakroom for depositing passengers' clothing. Access to the vestibule entrance is via an outward-opening double door between frames 12 and 14. One of the toilets is accessible from the vestibule by the left fuselage side wall, and the other likewise from the right fuselage side wall. Between them and the vestibule is the cloakroom intended for storing a portion of the passengers' clothing. For the crew, there is a small luggage space accessible by an opening hatch beneath the floor of the vestibule. By means of an outwards-opening door between frames 14 and 15 on the right fuselage side wall behind the toilet, the mail room of 3.5m³ (123.6ft³) can be entered. Behind this, also accessible through an outward-opening door between frames 15 and 16, is the load-trim room of 3.8m³ (134.2ft³) capacity, from which leads a door to the cloakroom deposi-tory and a door to the fuselage tail extremity, which is accessible in flight.

Top left: **Details of the kitchen or galley in the Ju 90 V4 (Handbook, Part 1).**

Top right: **The entrance vestibule in the rear fuselage area (Handbook, Part 1).**

Below: **Plan of the heating, de-icing and air-circulation systems (Handbook, Part 9).**

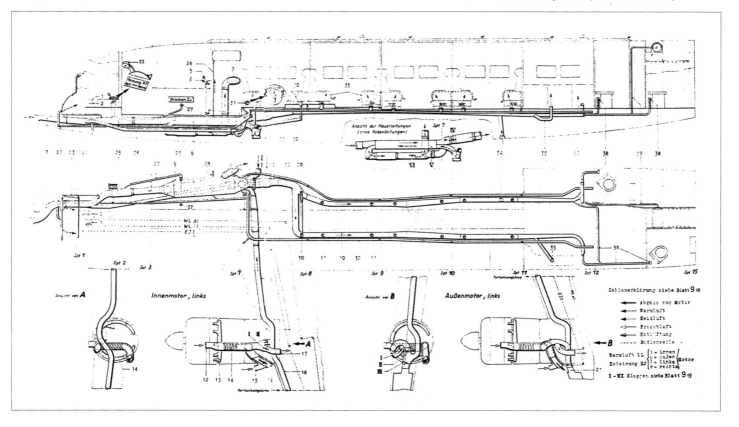

The Empennage

A further important construction assembly was the massive empennage area, consisting of twin endplate fins and rudders covered with smooth metal sheeting except for the corrugated sheet- covered rudder surfaces.

The fins and rudders, and tailplane and elevators, were covered on their leading edges with Conti rubber de-icing strips. The following original text and illustrations document the structural features of the empennage.

The Tailplane

Construction of the horizontal surfaces was as follows: The non-symmetrical 'double-wing' type of tailplane consists of the one-piece fixed horizontal surface and the two elevator halves. The cantilever tailplane, whose incidence can be adjusted in flight by the pilot, is moved by the hydraulic oil circuit. In its construction, it is a three-spar structure connected by ribs and transverse profiles, the whole covered with flat sheet metal. The tailplane is attached to the fuselage at Spar I to fuselage frame 19. For altering the angle of incidence, two adjustable pinions grip the diagonal struts I. The cut-out arising from the positioning of the tailplane on the rear fuselage is covered by an appropriate profile. For inspection of the airframe and the control rods situated in the tailplane, there are large flaps beneath the lower outer skin that are attached by screws with flush screwheads. For greasing the pendular lever, there are hand-opened covers fitted with snap-locks. Tailplane incidence can be adjusted between +2° and –3°, the normal position being +2°.

The Elevators

According to the Handbook, the construction and function of the elevators was as follows: The elevator is split into two halves, coupled together with an untwistable tube. The framework is comprised of two load-carrying spars connected by Z-shaped stringers. Its forward portion is covered with flush-riveted flat sheeting, the rear portion with corrugated sheet. On each half, the elevator is supported on three external strakes anchored by ball-bearings, that in the centre comprising a compensating

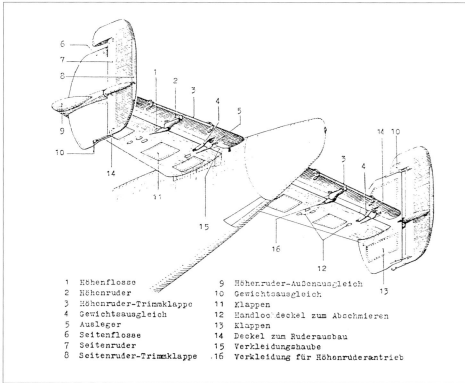

1	Höhenflosse	9	Höhenruder-Außenausgleich
2	Höhenruder	10	Gewichtsausgleich
3	Höhenruder-Trimmklappe	11	Klappen
4	Gewichtsausgleich	12	Handlochdeckel zum Abschmieren
5	Ausleger	13	Klappen
6	Seitenflosse	14	Deckel zum Ruderausbau
7	Seitenruder	15	Verkleidungshaube
8	Seitenruder-Trimmklappe	16	Verkleidung für Höhenruderantrieb

1	Lagerung
2	Lagerbolzen
3	Querverband I
4	Bolzen
5	Verstellspindel
6	Holzklotz

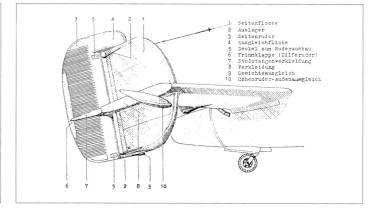

1	Seitenflosse
2	Ausleger
3	Seitenruder
4	Ausgleichfläche
5	Deckel zum Ruderausbau
6	Trimmklappe (Hilfsruder)
7	Stoßstangenverkleidung
8	Verkleidung
9	Gewichtsausgleich
10	Höhenruder-Außenausgleich

bearing. On each of the elevator halves, there are two compensating weights that balance the elevator weight by 100%. Each elevator additionally has an external compensating weight located outside the endplate fin. Elevator deflection is limited by stops in the tailplane and in the cockpit. At the trailing edge, each elevator has a servo-tab that independently serves to balance the forces and which, as a trim flap, can be operated from the cockpit.

The Fins

On the subject of the vertical surfaces, Part 3 of the Handbook gives the following information: The non-symmetrical twin fins and rudders comprise two tip-mounted surfaces. The cantilever fins are fixed by five universal screw joints to the tips of the tailplane. Constructionally, they are made up of three main load-carrying spars connected to each other by ribs and transverse profiles and covered with smooth sheet-metal. For inspection and maintenance purposes, on each inner side of the fins there are two large access panels. Through the removable skin panels between the fins and the elevator balances, access to the control rods is easily assured.

(As mentioned earlier, the V4 prototype was fitted for a limited period with a third, central fin.)

The Rudders

In its construction, each rudder is a three-spar structure connected by Z-shaped bracing. The forward portion is covered with smooth sheet-metal and the rear portion with corrugated sheet. Each endplate rudder is attached to the fin at three points containing ball-bearings, that in the middle being a compensating bearing. Rudder deflection is limited by stops in the fin and in the cockpit. By means of external compensating surfaces, the rudder weight is 100% balanced.

The Wing

This lift-providing element was laid out as a five-part, four-spar, low-positioned wing, the centre section of which was built as an integral part of the fuselage, this section containing four additional freight compartments with a total volume of 10m³ (353.1ft³). Each of the outer sections was connected by massive universal joints. The wing was of the Junkers 'double-wing' type of construction, with ailerons outermost and landing flaps on the inner sections, and housed a total of 4,400 litres of fuel. During the course of production, several types of powerplant were used, described in detail in a later section of this book. According to the Handbook, the wing comprised:

- Wing centre section
  (Tm = Tragflächen-Mittelstück)
- Wing mid or interim section
  (Tz = Tragflächen-Zwischenstück)
- Wing outer section (Tf = Außentragflächen).

Part 5 of the Handbook states: The cantilever wing has a positive leading-edge sweepback and is built in one piece integral with the fuselage, and together with the interim and outboard wing sections, comprises five main sub-assemblies. The wing interim sections have a negative, and the outer sections a positive, dihedral. The interim sections Tz are attached to the outer Tf and centre section Tm by universal joints. The gaps between the fuselage and the wing centre section Tm, and between the centre Tm and outer sections Tf, are covered by a space-fairing.

The outer wing sections are of the Junkers 'double-wing' type, consisting of the main fixed surfaces and the auxiliary surfaces moveable in flight. The latter are divided into outer and inner surfaces and both are able to serve as ailerons as well as landing flaps. A further landing aid are the split flaps at the rear of the wing centre section, used only in conjunction with the outer landing flaps.

The wing interim and outer sections each contain two fuel tanks, accessible via hatches on the wing underside. Additional covers and hatches serve for maintenance of internal parts as well as for work on wing components. Accessibility to wing internal spaces is afforded by manholes in the metal spars and ribs.

The wing leading edges are provided with warm-air circulation and heating so that ice formation is prevented. The warm air is provided from the four powerplants by two air heaters, which are connected to the exhaust gas circuit. In each of the warm air circuits, the heated air from both engines on one wing side are led via the outer engine into the leading-edge warm-air channel.

Wing Centre Section (Tm)

The wing centre section is built in one piece and is firmly attached to the fuselage side walls. The supporting elements are five spars whose upper and lower extremities consist of tubing. Where, at the outer connecting surfaces, it is not covered with flat sheet-metal ribs, it is sealed with fabric. The intermediate spaces of the spars from II up to the level of fuselage frame 10 are divided into three storage bays of 11m³ (388.4ft³) total capacity. Loading of the bays is from four ventrally-positioned lockable hatches.

Wing interim section (Tz)

The Tz is connected to the Tm by 12 universal ball-joints. The gaps between the Tz and the Tm and fuselage respectively are covered with space-fairings. Other than the five Tz spars, of

Right: **This wing planform was retained on the Ju 90 prototypes up to the V4 inclusive as well as for the mini-series.**

Photographs on the opposite page:

Top: **View of the port tail surfaces on Ju 90 D-ABDG Württemberg.**

Centre: **Details of the empennage (Handbook, Part 3). As on previous Junkers aircraft, the rudder and elevator surfaces were largely covered with corrugated sheet-metal.**

Bottom left: **The tailplane positioning points (Handbook, Part 3).**

Bottom right: **The starboard fin and rudder elements (Handbook, Part 3).**

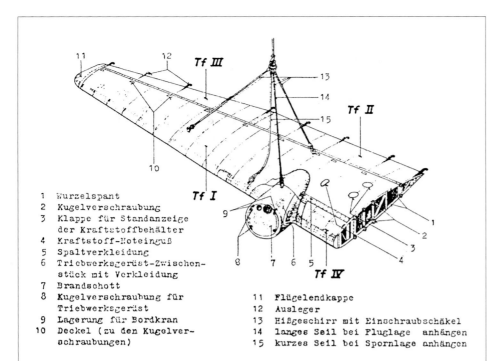

1	Wurzelspant
2	Kugelverschraubung
3	Klappe für Standanzeige der Kraftstoffbehälter
4	Kraftstoff-Noteinguß
5	Spaltverkleidung
6	Triebwerksgerüst-Zwischenstück mit Verkleidung
7	Brandschott
8	Kugelverschraubung für Triebwerksgerüst
9	Lagerung für Bordkran
10	Deckel (zu den Kugelverschraubungen)
11	Flügelendkappe
12	Ausleger
13	Hißgeschirr mit Einschraubschäkel
14	langes Seil bei Fluglage anhängen
15	kurzes Seil bei Spornlage anhängen

which the upper and lower extremities of the centre spar consist of T-shaped profiles, there are four additional auxiliary spars. One of these is a lattice-work truss, all others comprising metal-walled spars. Other than the root and outer tip ends, the Tz has two ribs between which the engine bulkhead and undercarriage supports are attached, the engine being attached to the bulkhead by four universal joints. The cowling on this interim section is firmly attached to the wing skinning by rivets.

Between spars 4 and 5 of the Tz there are two fuel tanks each of 480 litres capacity for cruising-flight fuel, and they can be removed from beneath the wing.

Wing outer section (Tf)

The outermost section is connected to the Tz by eight universal joints, the gap being covered by a space-fairing. The attachment point for the outboard engine is between ribs 2 and 3, where the engine is attached to the bulkhead by four universal joints. In the space between spars 4 and 5 there are two tanks each of 270 litres capacity housing the starting fuel, and these can be removed from beneath the wing.

Control Surfaces

The two-part ailerons consist of an outer and inner component and, together with the fixed wing, comprise the 'double-wing'. The forward portion of the ailerons consists of a rotatable anti-bending tube stiffened by ribs and covered with flat sheet-metal. The rear portion of the ailerons is purely fabric-covered.

There are five ball-bearing attachment points for the inner and outer ailerons, of which the centre three serve as balances. The inner as well as the outer ailerons can also function as hydraulically-operated flaps in the 'Start' [take-off or climb], 'Reise' [cruise], and 'Landung' [landing] positions. Accordingly the inner aileron is the inner flap and the outer aileron the outer flap. At a small angle of depression the take-off run can be appreciably shortened, while at a large angle the aircraft's glide angle can be so altered that a landing at a lower speed and landing run is possible.

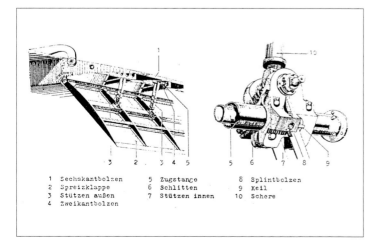

1	Endspant
2	Wurzelspant
3	Kugelverschraubungen
4	Triebwerksgerüst-Zwischenstück mit Verkleidung
5	Kugelverschraubung f. Triebwerksgerüst
6	Brandschott
7	Lagerung für Bordkran
8	Hißpunkte für gesamte Maschine
9	Kraftstoff-Noteinguß
10	Klappe für Standanzeige der Kraftstoffbehälter
11	Hißgeschirr für Tz

Above: **The starboard outer wing section (Tf) from Part 5 of the Handbook.**

Left: **An illustration from Part 5 of the Handbook showing the port interim wing section (Tz).**

Bottom left: **Details of the split flap and its mechanism (Handbook, Part 3).**

Bottom right: **Further details of the split flaps viewed from the front (Handbook, Part 3).**

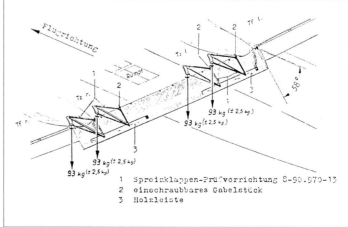

1	Sechskantbolzen
2	Spreizklappe
3	Stützen außen
4	Zweikantbolzen
5	Zugstange
6	Schlitten
7	Stützen innen
8	Splintbolzen
9	Keil
10	Schere

1	Spreizklappen-Prüfvorrichtung 8-98.970-13
2	einschraubbares Gabelstück
3	Holzleiste

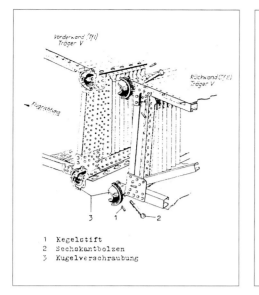

Vorderwand (Tf I)
Träger V

Rückwand (Tf II)
Träger V

Flugrichtung

1 Kegelstift
2 Sechskantbolzen
3 Kugelverschraubung

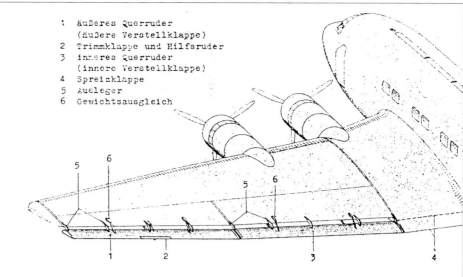

1 Äußeres Querruder
  (äußere Verstellklappe)
2 Trimmklappe und Hilfsruder
3 Inneres Querruder
  (innere Verstellklappe)
4 Spreizklappe
5 Ausleger
6 Gewichtsausgleich

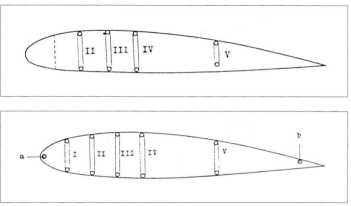

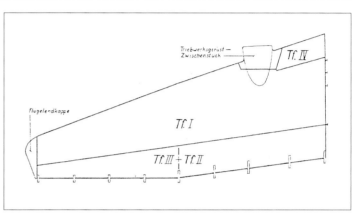

Triebwerksgerüst —
Zwischenstück

Tf. IV

Flügelendkappe

Tf. I

Tf. III + Tf. II

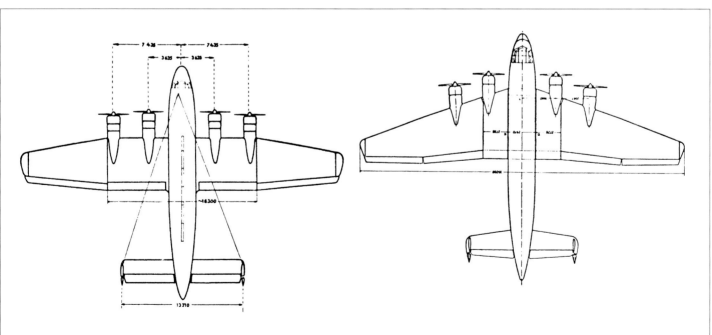

Top left: **Detail of the universal ball-joints on Spar V (starboard Tf), from the Handbook, Part 5.**

Top right: **Port-side aileron, trim-tab and flap surfaces (Handbook, Part 3).**

Centre left: **The upper drawing shows the universal ball-joints connecting the wing centre- and mid-sections (Tm and Tz), and the lower the mid- and outer-wing sections (Tz and Tf), from the Handbook, Part 5.**

Centre right: **The separate components of the outer wing section (Tf I to Tf IV).**

Bottom: **A comparison between the original Ju 90 wing planform (right) and that employed from the V5 prototype onwards.(left).**

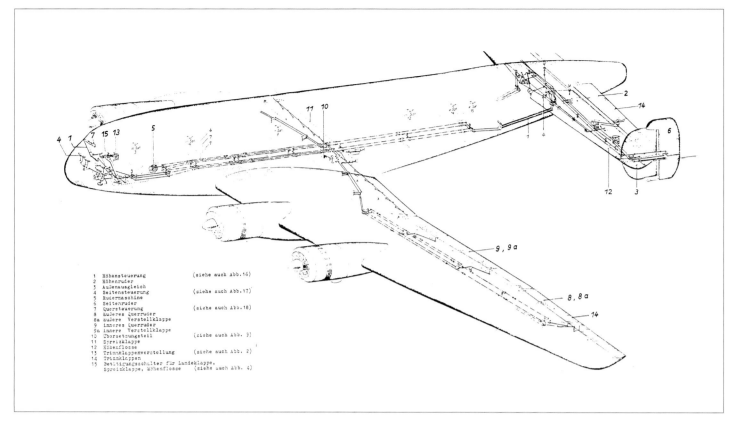

1	Höhensteuerung	(siehe auch Abb.16)
2	Höhenruder	
3	Außenausgleich	
4	Seitensteuerung	(siehe auch Abb.17)
5	Rudermaschine	
6	Seitenruder	
7	Quersteuerung	(siehe auch Abb.18)
8	äußeres Querruder	
8a	äußere Verstellklappe	
9	inneres Querruder	
9a	innere Verstellklappe	
10	Übersetzungsteil	(siehe auch Abb.3)
11	Spreizklappe	
12	Höhenflosse	
13	Trimmklappenverstellung	(siehe auch Abb.2)
14	Trimmklappen	
15	Betätigungsschalter für Landeklappe, Spreizklappe, Höhenflosse	(siehe auch Abb.4)

The control circuits of the Ju 90 (Handbook, Part 4).

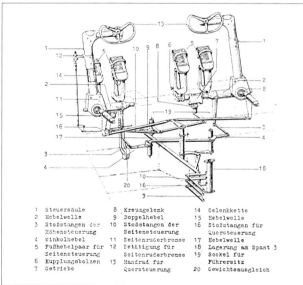

1	Steuersäule	8	Kreuzgelenk	14	Gelenkkette
2	Hebelwelle	9	Doppelhebel	15	Hebelwelle
3	Stoßstangen der Höhensteuerung	10	Stoßstangen der Seitensteuerung	16	Stoßstangen für Quersteuerung
4	Winkelhebel	11	Seitenruderbremse	17	Hebelwelle
5	Fußhebelpaar für Seitensteuerung	12	Betätigung für Seitenruderbremse	18	Lagerung am Spant 3
6	Kupplungsbolzen	13	Handrad für Quersteuerung	19	Sockel für Führersitz
7	Getriebe			20	Gewichtsausgleich

The control elements in the cockpit.

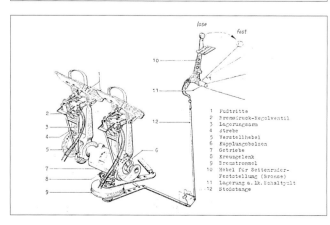

1	Fußtritte
2	Bremsdruck-Regelventil
3	Lagerungsarm
4	Strebe
5	Verstellhebel
6	Kupplungsbolzen
7	Getriebe
8	Kreuzgelenk
9	Bremstrommel
10	Hebel für Seitenruder-Feststellung (Bronze)
11	Lagerung a.lk.Schaltpult
12	Stoßstange

Details of the rudder mechanism.

Other Installations and Fittings

Besides its primary function of providing lift, the wing also served to house the fuel, the main undercarriage and an appreciable number of various other installations, consisting of:

- Fuel tanks (for positions and capacities see Technical Data Table)
- Fuel conduits
- Fuel pumps
- Tank content indicators
- Fuel drain-off
- Wing warm-air de-icing
- Fire-extinguisher system conduits
- Wing centre section loading bays of 11m³ (388.4ft³) capacity
- Engine supports ahead of firewalls on mid and outer sections
- Attachment for split flaps and Junkers 'double-wing' surfaces
- Position lights at the wingtips
- Landing lights beneath the outer wings
- Hoisting points for engine dismantling

These comprise the most important installations and fittings that were either housed or integrated into the wing structure.

The Controls

The equally comprehensive as well as complex control systems are illustrated here as they appeared in Part 4 of the Handbook.

The Main Undercarriage

During the often rough operations with such large aircraft, a massive and sturdy undercarriage was required. The maximum take-off weight of the Ju 90 varied according to its role, between 22,900kg (50,485 lb) and 26,700kg (58,863 lb). The Ju 290 V1 already exceeded the 40,000kg (88,184 lb) limit, and for this reason, as with various Ju 90 prototypes, it had twin-wheel main undercarriage units. The main undercarriage on the Ju 90, however, consisted of a forked undercarriage with only one mainwheel and oil/air shock absorption, with additional stability provided by V-shaped struts.

In the course of development, tyres of various dimensions were fitted. Examples were: 1450 x 500mm (57.1 x 19.7in) for the V1, 1650 x 600mm (65.0 x 23.6in) for the V4 and SAA aircraft, and 1320 x 480mm (52.0 x 18.9in) for the V5 to V8. The mainwheel track was 7.32m (24ft 0¼in).

Equipping the Ju 90 with a tailwheel was undoubtedly not a compelling design feature. At that time aircraft with nosewheel undercarriages were the exception, and the practice was shunned as an American innovation. Upon looking more closely at this topic, it becomes evident that the nosewheel undercarriage was without doubt an American feature, and numerous examples are to be found, both of fighters and bombers and in the transport category, such as the Douglas C-54/DC-4 series and the Lockheed C-69 Constellation, but not the Boeing Stratoliner, as it was closely related to the B-17 bomber. In other countries, such as France, Great Britain and the Soviet Union, development of aircraft with this feature was less notable – as was also the case in Germany. The nosewheel was limited in the main to aircraft such as the Do 335, He 162, He 219, Ta 154, Me 262 and Me 264. Several German experimental and/or limited-production aircraft (including civil and military transports) were also built with a nosewheel undercarriage, namely the Arado Ar 232 and Ar 234B and C; Focke-Achgelis Fa 223 helicopter; Göppingen Gö 9; Heinkel He 176 and He 280; Horten H VII and H IX; Gotha Go 242 and Go 244; Kalkert Ka 430; Junkers Ju 248 (Me 263) and Ju 287; Lippisch DM-1; and the Messerschmitt Bf 109 V23, Me 163D, Me 309 and Me 321. Additionally, several prototypes under construction with a nosewheel undercarriage, such as the Blohm & Voss Bv 144, DFS P.1068, Heinkel He 343, Henschel Hs 132, Lippisch P.11 V1 and Messerschmitt P.1101 V1, among others, did not reach the flight-test stage at the end of the war. However, none of the German transport aircraft actually realised were fitted with this useful component.

Illustrations of the rolling components of the Ju 90 are provided in the Ju 90Z Handbook, Part 2. Here, the drawings but not the corresponding text are used to provide a picture of the technicalities in this area.

Note the somewhat despondent look of this youngster, posing reluctantly in front of the Ju 90 mainwheel, which measured 1450 x 500mm (57.1 x 19.7in).

Details of the Ju 90's port main undercarriage (Handbook, Part 2).

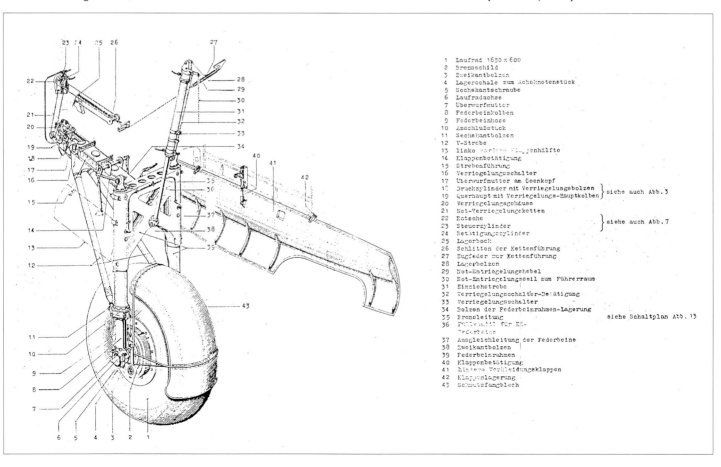

1 Laufrad 1650 x 600
2 Bremsschild
3 Zweikantbolzen
4 Lagerschale zum Achsknotenstück
5 Sechskantschraube
6 Laufradachse
7 Überwurfmutter
8 Federbeinkolben
9 Federbeinhose
10 Anschlußstück
11 Sechskantbolzen
12 V-Strebe
13 linke vordere Flügenhälfte
14 Klappenbetätigung
15 Strebenführung
16 Verriegelungsschalter
17 Überwurfmutter am Ösenkopf
18 Druckzylinder mit Verriegelungsbolzen } siehe auch Abb.3
19 Querhaupt mit Verriegelungs-Hauptkolben
20 Verriegelungsgehäuse
21 Not-Verriegelungsketten
22 Ratsche } siehe auch Abb.7
23 Steuerzylinder
24 Betätigungszylinder
25 Lagerbock
26 Schlitten der Kettenführung
27 Zugfeder zur Kettenführung
28 Lagerbolzen
29 Not-Entriegelungshebel
30 Not-Entriegelungsseil zum Führerraum
31 Einziehstrebe
32 Verriegelungsschalter-Betätigung
33 Verriegelungsschalter
34 Bolzen der Federbeinrahmen-Lagerung
35 Bremsleitung siehe Schaltplan Abb. 13
36 Füllventil für Ex-Federbeine
37 Ausgleichleitung der Federbeine
38 Zweikantbolzen
39 Federbeinrahmen
40 Klappenbetätigung
41 hintere Verkleidungsklappen
42 Klappenlagerung
43 Schmutzfangblech

The Tailwheel

The following commentary, taken from the Handbook, Part 2, explains the construction of this portion of the aircraft. The retractable tailwheel installed was of various dimensions, for example 875 x 320mm (34.4 x 12.6in).

Like the two halves of the mainwheel undercarriage, the hydraulically operated tailwheel situated at the fuselage rear between frames 20 and 22 has a sprung suspension. It consists of the wheel, a wheel fork, sprung wheel lever, EC shock-absorber oleo-leg, and the retraction

mechanism. From the cockpit, the swivel wheel is rotatable through 360° and, by means of a hand lever, can be anchored to the oleo-leg lever. The tailwheel, a one-piece Electron cast with a deep-bedded rim, is fitted with ball-bearings. The balloon-type (strengthened) tyre of 780 x 260mm [30.7 x 10.2in] has a tyre pressure of 4atm.

The Powerplants

Since it powered the overwhelming majority of the Ju 90s built, preference will be given to the BMW 132, chosen because Daimler-Benz engines were not available for civilian use, so recourse had to be made to the products of other manufacturers. Up to 1928 BMW had only made in-line engines, but this changed radically with the granting of a licence agreement with the American Pratt & Whitney company. The agreement was for licence manufacture of the Hornet B nine-cylinder radial, which went into production as the Hornet A. In 1933 BMW secured the licensing rights for the further developed Hornet, which was converted to German standards and metric measurements. The previously used priming system for three and five cylinders was replaced by a nine-cylinder system. Additionally, this motor featured an

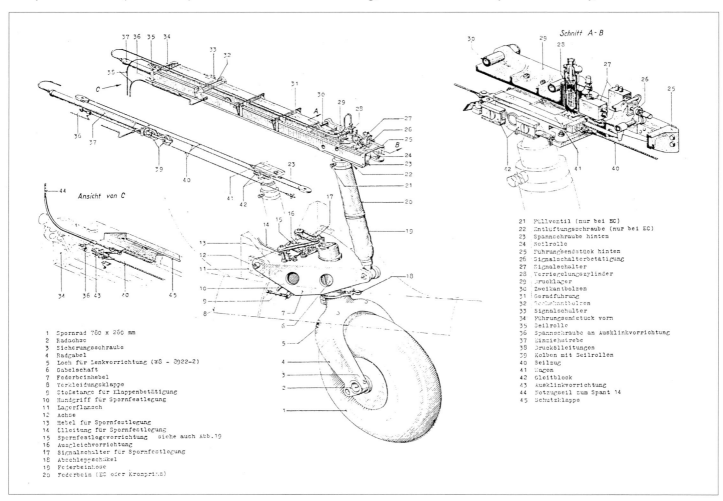

1   Spornrad 780 x 260 mm
2   Radachse
3   Sicherungsschraube
4   Radgabel
5   Loch für Lenkvorrichtung (WS - 3922-2)
6   Gabelschaft
7   Federbeinhebel
8   Verkleidungsklappe
9   Stoßstange für Klappenbetätigung
10 Handgriff für Spornfestlegung
11 Lagerflansch
12 Achse
13 Hebel für Spornfestlegung
14 Ölleitung für Spornfestlegung
15 Spornfestlegevorrichtung   siehe auch Abb.19
16 Ausgleichvorrichtung
17 Signalschalter für Spornfestlegung
18 Abschleppschäkel
19 Federbeinhose
20 Federbein (EC oder Kronprinz)

21 Füllventil (nur bei EC)
22 Entlüftungsschraube (nur bei EC)
23 Spannschraube hinten
24 Seilrolle
25 Führungsendstück hinten
26 Signalschalterbetätigung
27 Signalschalter
28 Verriegelungszylinder
29 Drucklager
30 Zweikantbolzen
31 Geradführung
32 Sechskantbolzen
33 Signalschalter
34 Führungsendstück vorn
35 Seilrolle
36 Spannschraube an Ausklinkvorrichtung
37 Einziehstrebe
38 Drucköilleitungen
39 Kolben mit Seilrollen
40 Seilzug
41 Wagen
42 Gleitblock
43 Ausklinkvorrichtung
44 Notzugseil zum Spant 14
45 Schutzklappe

Detail views of the BMW 132 radial from various perspectives.

Photographs on the opposite page:

Top: **A scene beneath this giant airliner. Besides the undercarriage details, the openings for the underfloor storage hatches are visible. In the background is Ju 90Z-2 D-ABDG *Württemberg*.**

Bottom: **Details of the Ju 90's retractable tailwheel (Handbook, Part 2).**

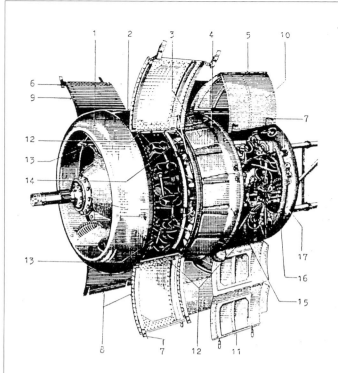

1	vorderer Strömungsring
2	vorderer Verkleidungsring
3	Spreizklappenring
4	Schild
5	hinterer Verkleidungsring
6	Hebelverschluß
7	Sicherungsdeckel
8	untere Klappen
9	obere Klappen
10	obere Klappen, hinten
11	untere Klappen, hinten
12	Gelenkband
13	Befestigungsstange
14	Stütze
15	Schildsegment
16	Endspant
17	Brandspant

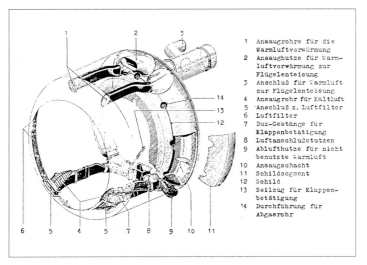

1 Ansaugrohre für die Warmluftvorwärmung
2 Ansaughutze für Warmluftvorwärmung zur Flügelenteisung
3 Anschluß für Warmluft zur Flügelenteisung
4 Ansaugrohr für Kaltluft
5 Anschluß z. Luftfilter
6 Luftfilter
7 Duz-Gestänge für Klappenbetätigung
8 Luftanschlußstutzen
9 Ablufthutze für nicht benutzte Warmluft
10 Ansaugschacht
11 Schildsegment
12 Schild
13 Seilzug für Klappenbetätigung
14 Durchführung für Abgasrohr

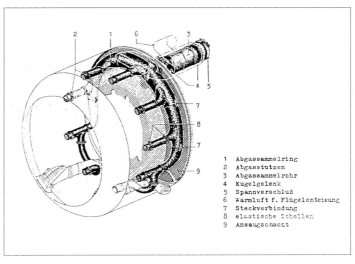

1 Abgassammelring
2 Abgasstutzen
3 Abgassammelrohr
4 Kugelgelenk
5 Spannverschluß
6 Warmluft f. Flügelenteisung
7 Steckverbindung
8 elastische Schellen
9 Ansaugschacht

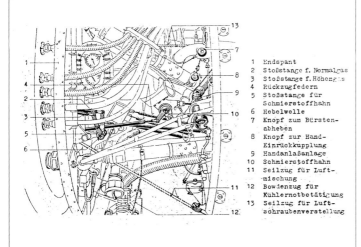

1 Endspant
2 Stoßstange f. Normalgas
3 Stoßstange f. Höhengas
4 Rückzugfedern
5 Stoßstange für Schmierstoffhahn
6 Hebelwelle
7 Knopf zum Bürstenabheben
8 Knopf zur Hand-Einrückkupplung
9 Handanlaßanlage
10 Schmierstoffhahn
11 Seilzug für Luftmischung
12 Bowdenzug für Kühlernotbetätigung
13 Seilzug für Luftschraubenverstellung

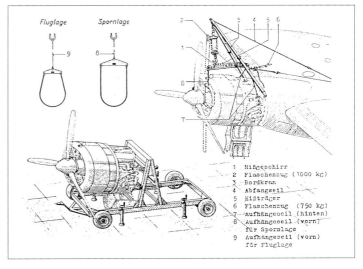

1 Hißgeschirr
2 Flaschenzug (1000 kg)
3 Bordkran
4 Abfangseil
5 Hißträger
6 Flaschenzug (750 kg)
7 Aufhängeseil (hinten)
8 Aufhängeseil (vorn) für Spornlage
9 Aufhängeseil (vorn) für Fluglage

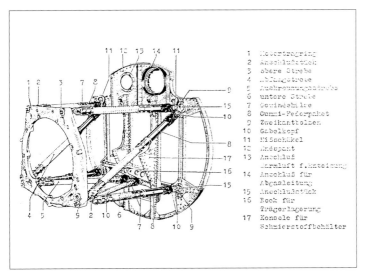

1 Motortragring
2 Anschlußstück
3 obere Strebe
4 Abfangstrebe
5 Anschraubungsstrebe
6 untere Strebe
7 Gewindehülse
8 Gummi-Federpaket
9 Zweikantbolzen
10 Gabelkopf
11 Hißschäkel
12 Endspant
13 Anschluß Warmluft f. Enteisung
14 Anschluß für Abgasleitung
15 Anschlußstück
16 Bock für Trägerlagerung
17 Konsole für Schmierstoffbehälter

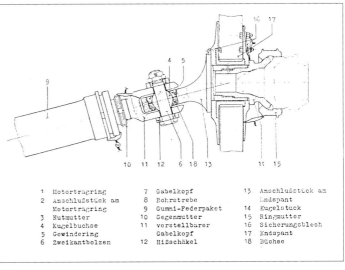

1 Motortragring
2 Anschlußstück am Motortragring
3 Nutmutter
4 Kugelbuchse
5 Gewindering
6 Zweikantbolzen
7 Gabelkopf
8 Rohrstrebe
9 Gummi-Federpaket
10 Gegenmutter
11 verstellbarer Gabelkopf
12 Hißschäkel
13 Anschlußstück am Endspant
14 Kugelstück
15 Ringmutter
16 Sicherungsblech
17 Endspant
18 Büchse

Photographs on the opposite page:

Top left: **This scene was photographed on 13th July 1938 at Berlin-Tempelhof, when four mechanics were able to exchange the BMW 132H/1 within 25 minutes – a useful subject for the diorama modeller, perhaps.**

Centre left: **The same scene from a different perspective.**

Top right: **The BMW 132H/1 inspection and maintenance openings (Handbook, Part 6).**

Bottom left: **Frontal view of the BMW 132H/1 quick-change engine.**

Bottom right: **Rear view of the BMW 132H/1 with its carburettors and compressors.**

Photographs on this page:

Illustrations from the BA 132 H/1 Handbook showing (top left) air-intake details, (top right) exhaust-gas circuit, (centre left) various components, (centre right) engine removal and transport, (bottom left) engine support frames, and (bottom right) engine attachment to the rear wall.

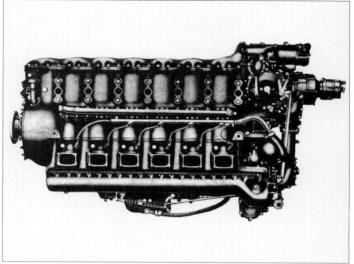

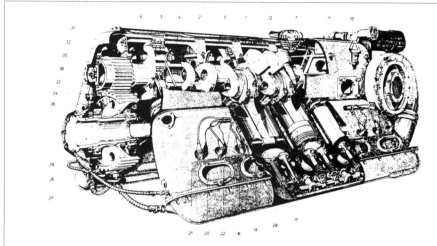

1 Kurbelgehäuse
2 Kurbelwelle
3 Hauptlager
4 Lagerbrücke
5 Schmierstoffkanal
6 Kurbelgehäusedeckel
7 Entlüftung
10 Aufhängeflansch

11 Heißöse
16 Pleuel
17 Kolben
18 Laufbuchse
20 Auspuffflansch
21 Zündkerze
22 Schraubring
28 Zylinderkopfdeckel

29 Propellerwelle
30 Getrieberitzel
31 u. 32 Lager
34 Stirnrad
35, 36 u. 37 Lager
38 Schmierstoffverteiler

exhaust-gas preheating system developed by BMW. The BMW 123A and E delivered up to 660hp, and in the course of development further versions based on the A appeared, these consisting of the BMW 132T, Y and Z. All these models, including the D, were equipped with carburettors, while the G and L sub-types were of 725hp and 830hp respectively.

The culmination of the BMW 132 series was the introduction of the Einheitstriebwerk (all-in-one engine) or Schnellwechseltriebwerk (quick-change engine). The BMW 132H could be exchanged as a complete unit, that is with all the components, including the lubricant tank, necessary for engine operation. All the conduits running inside the Ju 90 fuselage were therefore concentrated into a single channel accessible from the outside. This novelty enabled safe and speedy access to the cables and fuel-feed lines between the engines, wings

and fuselage. A system was thus evolved that enabled a complete engine to be changed in less than 30 minutes, and during a demonstration held in Berlin-Tempelhof on 13th July 1938, the port side inner engine of the DLH *Bayern*, with a trained four-man team, was changed in 25 minutes. Lufthansa also successfully adopted this principle for its Focke-Wulf Condor.

In brief, the most important details of the BMW 132H/1 were:

- Layout: nine-cylinder radial of 27.72 litres (1,690in³) cylinder capacity, bore 155.5mm (6.12in), stroke 162mm (6.38in), and compression ratio 6.5:1
- Max power: 1,000hp at 2,550rpm (100 octane)
- Continuous power: 690hp at 2,090rpm
- Cruising power: 560hp at 2,000rpm
- Fuel consumption: 220gm per hp/hr (87 octane)

Top left: **The DB 600 powerplant of the Ju 89 and Ju 90 V1.**

Top right: **Side view of the Jumo 211.**

Above left: **A cutaway drawing of the DB 600 12-cylinder inverted-V in-line engine.**

Above right: **Internal details of the Jumo 211F 12-cylnder in-line engine, installed later on in the Ju 90 V4.**

Further versions of the much-used BMW 132 appeared, including the F, J, K, M, N, P, U and S, which had a direct injection system. These were used exclusively as high-altitude engines with transmission gearing. According to works records, up to April 1940 a total of 13,246 examples of all versions had been delivered at a cost of RM 22,000 per unit.

Top left: **The Ju 90 V6 was powered by the BMW 139, of which only a few were built.**

Centre and bottom left: **The BMW 801A was installed in the Ju 90 V7 and V8. The 801A, D, E and L models were standard installations in the Ju 290.**

Top and centre right: **The Pratt & Whitney Twin Wasp radial, which produced 1,200hp at take-off and 910hp at maximum continuous power, was installed in the two Ju 90s (Werknummern 900002 and 900004) ordered by SAA.**

Bottom right: **Calculations were also made using the Wright Cyclone radial as a basis. This particular motor was used, for example, in the Boeing 307.**

Technical Data of the BMW 132 H/1

Powerplant Data

Engine layout	nine-cylinder radial
Bore	155.5mm (6.12in)
Stroke	162.0mm (6.38in)
Cylinder capacity (each)	3.076 litres (187.7in³)
Cylinder capacity (total)	27.72 litres (1,690in³)
Compression ratio	6.5:1
Intake and exhaust valves	one each on intake and exhaust side
Spark plugs	Bosch DW 240ET 3/l or Siemens 30 FA 14D
Ignition sequence	1-3-5-7-9-2-4-6-8
Ignition system	2 x Bosch GE9 BLS 155/156
Starter unit	Bosch Eclipse ALISGC 24L2
Working method	Inertia starter
Power generator	Bosch LK 1200/24 CL
Reduction gear	0.62 via bevel wheel rotary drive
Carburettor type	Pallas Stromberg suction-type, Model NAY-9-A

Performance Data

Increased short-duration power at sea-level	1,000hp (100 octane), 880hp (87 octane), at 2,500rpm; 1-min limit
Increased short-duration power at 300m (984ft)	1,010hp (100 octane) at 2,500rpm; 1-minute limit
Increased short-duration power at 600m (1,968ft)	900hp (87 octane) at 2,500rpm; 1-minute limit
Short-duration power at sea-level	800hp at 2,250rpm; 5-minute limit
Short-duration power at 1,100m (3,610ft)	830hp at 2,250rpm; 5-minute limit
Continuous power at sea-level	640hp at 2,090rpm; no limit
Increased continuous power at sea-level	720hp at 2,180rpm; 30-minute limit
Increased continuous power at 1,550m (5,085ft)	760hp at 2,180rpm; 30-minute limit
Cruising power at 2,500m (8,200ft)	615hp at 2,000rpm; no limit

Fuel and Lubricant Consumption

Fuel consumption	270-300gm per hp/hr (short-duration)
Fuel consumption	230-260gm per hp/hr (continuous power)
Cruising consumption	220-235gm per hp/hr
Lubricant consumption	1-6kg/hr (mean value 2-4kg/hr)
Lubricant	Intava Rotring or Intava 100 M

Dimensions and Weights

Motor length	1,217mm (47.91in)
Motor diameter	1,380mm (54.33in)
Dry weight	530kg (1,168 lb)
Installation weight	1,050kg (2,315 lb) with cowling and airscrews

Another powerplant used in the Ju 90-series was the BMW 139, which consisted of two BMW 132s, but which had no future. This twin-row radial had a total cylinder capacity of 41.2 litres (2,524in³) and delivered up to 1,550hp. However, the only Ju 90 to be equipped with it was the V6, and its unreliability made several exchanges necessary. For the two machines ordered by SAA, US engines were specified: the 14-cylinder Pratt & Whitney Twin Wasp of 29.98 litres (1,830in³) capacity intended for installation produced 1,200hp at take-off. The V7 and V8 had much larger powerplants; with these prototypes progressive steps were taken in several areas, including the engines, to pave the way to the Ju 290. These two prototypes were powered by the BMW 801A of 41.8 litres (2,551in³) cylinder capacity and 1,560hp take-off power. A quick overview of the various powerplants installed in the Ju 90 is as follows:

- Ju 89   DB 600C
- Ju 90 V1   DB 600A
- Ju 90 V2   BMW 132H/1
- Ju 90 V3   BMW 132H/1
- Ju 90 V4   BMW 132H/1. Jumo 211F in 1941. Also considered was 1,200hp 12-cylinder BMW 800, development of which was terminated
- Ju 90 V5   BMW 132M
- Ju 90 V6   BMW 139. Due to problems with this still immature unit, several engine changes were necessary. Conversion of this airframe to the BMW 801 was not carried out as the V6 fuselage was used for the prototype Ju 290 V1.
- Ju 90 V7   BMW 801A
- Ju 90 V8   BMW 801A
- Ju 90 0001   BMW 132H/1
- Ju 90 0002   P&W SC-G Twin Wasp
- Ju 90 0003   BMW 132H/1
- Ju 90 0004   P&W SC-G Twin Wasp
- Ju 90 0005   BMW 132H/1.

Technical Data for the Jumo 211F, DB 600A, BMW 139, BMW 801A and Pratt & Whitney SC-G

	Jumo 211F	DB 600A	BMW 139	BMW 801A	Pratt & Whitney SC-G
Powerplant Data					
No of cylinders	12	12	14	14	14
Arrangement	inverted-V	inverted-V	2-row radial	2-row radial	2-row radial
Cylinder volume (total)	34.97 litres (2,134in³)	33.9 litres (2,069in³)	41.2 litres (2,514in³)	41.8 litres (2,551in³)	24.99 litres (1,830in³)
Cylinder volume (each)	2.914 litres (177.9in³)	2.825 litres (172.4in³)	2.94 litres (179.4in³)	2.985 litres (182.2in³)	2.14 litres (130.7in³)
Bore	150mm (5.91in)	150mm (5.91in)	155.5mm (6.12in)	156mm (6.14in)	140mm (5.51in)
Stroke	165mm (6.50in)	160mm (6.30in)	155mm (6.10in)	156mm (6.14in)	140mm (5.51in)
Compression ratio	6.5	6.5	6.5	6.5	6.7
Supercharger type	2-speed	s-l blower	2-speed	2-speed	2-speed
Cooling type	water/glycol	water	air	air	air
Performance					
Take-off power	1,340hp at 2,600rpm	1,000hp at 2,400rpm	1,500hp at 2,700rpm	1,600hp at 2,700rpm	1,200hp at 2,700rpm
Fuel consumption	226gm per hp/hr	292gm per hp/hr	225gm per hp/hr	205gm per hp/hr	215gm per hp/hr
Rated altitude	5,300m (17,390ft)	sea-level	5,400m (17,715ft)	4,600m (15,090ft)	-
Dimensions and Weights					
Motor length	2,173mm (85.6in)	1,720mm (67.7in)	1,558mm (61.3in)	2,006mm (79.0in)	1,593mm (62.7in)
Width or diameter	804mm (31.7in)	712mm (28.0in)	1,300mm (51.2in)	1,290mm (50.8in)	1,221mm (48.1in)
Height	1,053mm (41.5in)	1,000mm (39.4in)	-	-	-
Dry weight	720kg (1,587 lb)	545kg (1,202 lb)	850kg (1,874 lb)	1,010kg (2,227 lb)	662kg (1,460 lb)

The Fuel, Lubricant and Cooling Systems

The Ju 90 fuel system was extensive and, because of the requirements set, complex. Numerous pumps, valves, conduits and other equipment enabled filling and fuel transfer to the powerplants according to their appropriate needs. The Handbook text and illustrations document the set-up, referring to the wing centre section (Tm), interim sections (Tz) and outboard sections (Tf).

In each of the wing centre sections there are two fuel tanks holding 620 litres for cruising flight fuel. Additionally, each of the detachable outer wing sections houses an auxiliary cruising fuel tank, divided in two compartments each containing 210 litres. The Tz tanks and Tf tanks (cruising flight fuel) thus have a total capacity of 4 x 620 + 4 x 210 = 3,320 litres. Each outer wing section further contains two fuel tanks, each of 270 litres capacity, making a total of 4 x 270 = 1,080 litres, comprising take-off fuel of higher octane content. The Tf and Tz fuel tanks are fixed in position by tension bands and secured by arrester belts, and can be removed after these have been detached.

Tank filling for both types of fuel takes place from pressure-feed openings accessible beneath a flap that covers the filling connection ports in each wing interim section. At these positions are also the fuel quick-release installations. The conduits leading from the tanks to the filling connections and N3V batteries consist of Avio-tub hoses. Fuel tank ventilation on each wing half is by means of a common ventilation circuit.

The lubricant tanks, of 88 litres total capacity, contain 66 litres of lubricant and are located at the end bulkhead between the two upper connecting stations of the powerplant supporting frames. These are positioned on two shelves and fixed by tension bands. Within each tank there is a filling limiter that comes into action as soon as each tank contains the prescribed 66 litres.

For regulating the lubricant temperature, the lubrication system has a thermostat-controlled cooler that can be extended and retracted by an electromotor. The lubricant cooler's movable motor consists of a strengthened LMOT 45 of 125W power, a worm drive, and the shaft, together with the associated components. The motor's high rotational speed is reduced by the worm drive and the shaft to a lower value.

Below: **Fuel tank positions and circuitry. Differences existed between the Ju 90 V4 and 900001/900003 (Handbook, Part 7).**

Bottom left: **The fuel tanks in the wing interim section Tz (Handbook, Part 7).**

Bottom right: **Location of the Jumo fuel pumps (Handbook, BA BMW 132 H/1).**

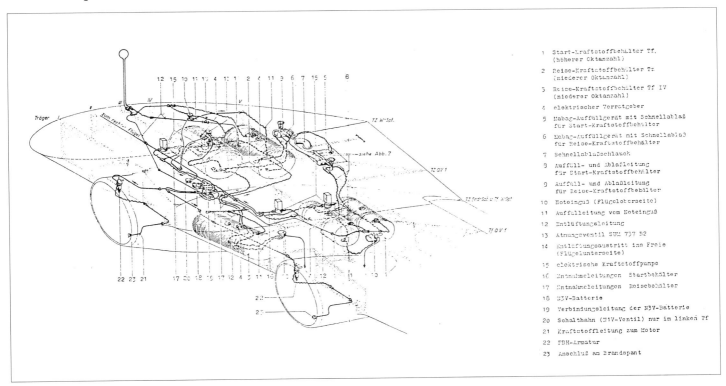

1 Start-Kraftstoffbehälter Tf,
   (höherer Oktanzahl)
2 Reise-Kraftstoffbehälter Tz
   (niederer Oktanzahl)
3 Reise-Kraftstoffbehälter Tf IV
   (niederer Oktanzahl)
4 elektrischer Vorratgeber
5 Mabag-Auffüllgerät mit Schnellablaß
   für Start-Kraftstoffbehälter
6 Mabag-Auffüllgerät mit Schnellablaß
   für Reise-Kraftstoffbehälter
7 Schnellablaßschlauch
8 Auffüll- und Ablaßleitung
   für Start-Kraftstoffbehälter
9 Auffüll- und Ablaßleitung
   für Reise-Kraftstoffbehälter
10 Noteinguß (Flügeloberseite)
11 Auffülleitung vom Noteinguß
12 Entlüftungsleitung
13 Atmungsventil SUM 737 B2
14 Entlüftungsaustritt ins Freie
   (Flügelunterseite)
15 elektrische Kraftstoffpumpe
16 Entnahmeleitungen Startbehälter
17 Entnahmeleitungen Reisebehälter
18 N3V-Batterie
19 Verbindungsleitung der N3V-Batterie
20 Schalthahn (N1V-Ventil) nur im linken Tf
21 Kraftstoffleitung zum Motor
22 FBH-Armatur
23 Anschluß am Brandspant

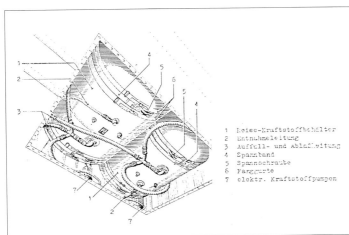

1 Reise-Kraftstoffbehälter
2 Entnahmeleitung
3 Auffüll- und Ablaßleitung
4 Spannband
5 Spannschraube
6 Fanggurte
7 elektr. Kraftstoffpumpen

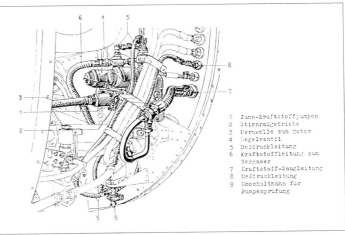

1 Jumo-Kraftstoffpumpen
2 Stirnradgetriebe
3 Fernwelle zum Motor
4 Kegelventil
5 Meßdruckleitung
6 Kraftstoffleitung zum
   Vergaser
7 Kraftstoff-Saugleitung
8 Meßdruckleitung
9 Umschalthahn für
   Pumpenprüfung

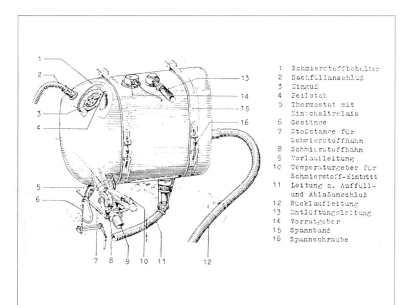

1 Schmierstoffbehälter
2 Nachfüllanschluß
3 Einguß
4 Peilstab
5 Thermostat mit Einschaltrelais
6 Gestänge
7 Stoßstange für Schmierstoffhahn
8 Schmierstoffhahn
9 Vorlaufleitung
10 Temperaturgeber für Schmierstoff-Eintritt
11 Leitung z. Auffüll- und Ablaßanschluß
12 Rücklaufleitung
13 Entlüftungsleitung
14 Vorratgeber
15 Spannband
16 Spannschraube

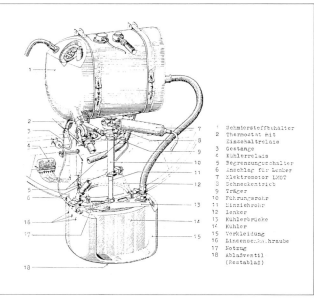

1 Schmierstoffbehälter
2 Thermostat mit Einschaltrelais
3 Gestänge
4 Kühlerrelais
5 Begrenzungsschalter
6 Anschlag für Lenker
7 Elektromotor LMOT
8 Schneckentrieb
9 Träger
10 Führungsrohr
11 Einziehrohr
12 Lenker
13 Kühlerbrücke
14 Kühler
15 Verkleidung
16 Linsenschraube
17 Notzug
18 Ablaßventil (Restablaß)

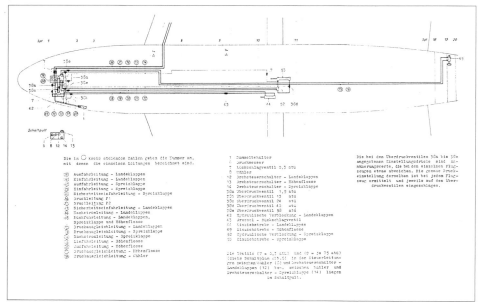

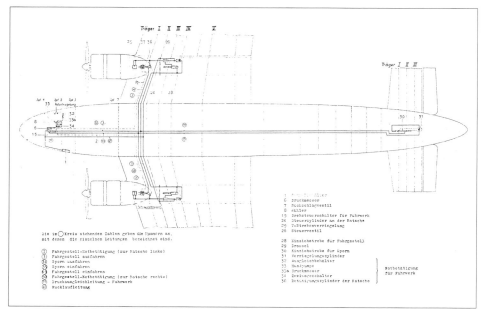

▼ Nach je 10 Flugstunden

Abschmieren der Blattwurzellager durch die Fettpreßnippel in der Nabe mit

Mobil-Compound-Öl Nr.2.

Bei kaltem Wetter Mobil-Compound-Öl Nr.1 oder Rizinusöl.

□ Nach je 25 Flugstunden

Abschrauben der Deckel an Fliehgewichten und die bananenförmigen Kugellager der Verstellarme mit demselben Öl abschmieren.

Prüfvorschrift

Nach je 100 Flugstunden

Ausbau der Luftschraube, zerlegen und Einzelteile prüfen (siehe Handbuch für Verstelluftschraube).

Top left: **The 66-litre lubricant tank (Handbook, BA 132 H/1).**

Top right: **The lubricant cooler could be extended or retracted by the movable motor to the desired position (Handbook, BA 132 H/1).**

Above: **The Junkers-Hamilton variable-pitch airscrews (Handbook, Flugbetrieb – Flying Operations).**

Centre left: **Layout of the hydraulic circuits in the fuselage (Handbook, Part 4).**

Left: **The undercarriage hydraulic circuits (Handbook, Part 2).**

Opposite page: **Layout of the electrical installations (Handbook, Part 9).**

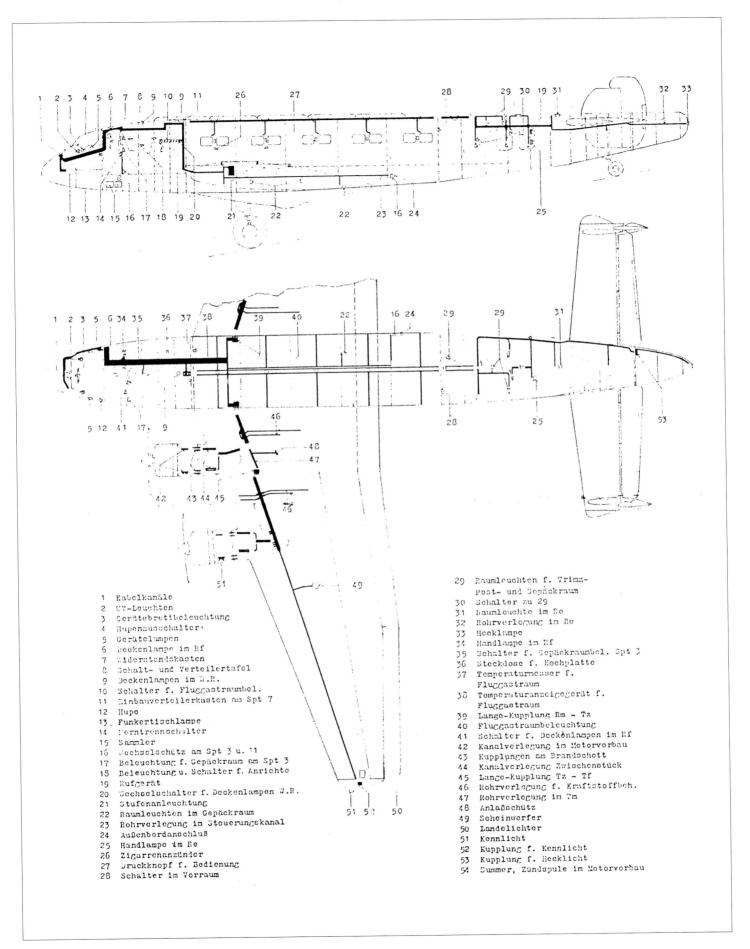

1   Kabelkanäle
2   UV-Leuchten
3   Gerätebrettbeleuchtung
4   Hupenausschalter
5   Gerätelampen
6   Deckenlampe im Hf
7   Widerstandskasten
8   Schalt- und Verteilertafel
9   Deckenlampen im W.R.
10 Schalter f. Fluggastraumbel.
11 Einbauverteilerkasten am Spt 7
12 Hupe
13 Funkertischlampe
14 Ferntrennschalter
15 Sammler
16 Wechselschütz am Spt 3 u. 11
17 Beleuchtung f. Gepäckraum am Spt 3
18 Beleuchtung u. Schalter f. Anrichte
19 Rufgerät
20 Wechselschalter f. Deckenlampen W.R.
21 Stufenanleuchtung
22 Raumleuchten im Gepäckraum
23 Rohrverlegung im Steuerungskanal
24 Außenbordanschluß
25 Handlampe im Re
26 Zigarrenanzünder
27 Druckknopf f. Bedienung
28 Schalter im Vorraum

29 Raumleuchten f. Trimm-
    Post- und Gepäckraum
30 Schalter zu 29
31 Raumleuchte im Re
32 Rohrverlegung im Re
33 Hecklampe
34 Handlampe im Hf
35 Schalter f. Gepäckraumbel. Spt 3
36 Steckdose f. Kochplatte
37 Temperaturmesser f.
    Fluggastraum
38 Temperaturanzeigegerät f.
    Fluggastraum
39 Lange-Kupplung Rm – Tz
40 Fluggastraumbeleuchtung
41 Schalter f. Deckenlampen im Hf
42 Kanalverlegung im Motorvorbau
43 Kupplungen am Brandschott
44 Kanalverlegung Zwischenstück
45 Lange-Kupplung Tz – Tf
46 Rohrverlegung f. Kraftstoffbeh.
47 Rohrverlegung im Tm
48 Anlaßschütz
49 Scheinwerfer
50 Landelichter
51 Kennlicht
52 Kupplung f. Kennlicht
53 Kupplung f. Hecklicht
54 Summer, Zündspule im Motorvorbau

73

Ju 90Z-2 Technical Data

Fuselage

Overall length	26.45m (86ft 9⅜in)
Maximum height (nose)	6.55m (21ft 5⅞in)
Maximum height (to fin tips)	7.30m (23ft 11⅜in)
No of transverse frames	24
Type of construction	all-metal semi-monocoque
Covering	flat sheeting

Fuselage main assemblies

Cockpit area	Frames 1 to 3
Forward storage space	Frames 3 to 7; 6.7m³ (236.6ft³) capacity
Passenger cabins	Frames 7 to 12 (including three storage areas of 10m³ capacity)
Rear usable space	Frames 12 to 14 (including baggage room)
Mail room	Frames 14 to 15; 3.5m³ (123.6ft³) capacity
Load-trim room	Frames 15 to 16; 3.8m³ (134.2ft³) capacity

Wing

Main assemblies	5 segments (1 Tm, 2 Tz, 2 Tf sections)
Overall span	35.02m (114ft 10¾in)
Wing area	184m² (1,980.51ft²)
Root chord (maximum)	7.57m (24ft 10in)
Mean wing chord	5.88m (19ft 3½in)
Tip chord	2.34m (7ft 8⅛in)
Aspect ratio	6.67
Wing loading (at max weight)	126.6kg/m² (25.93 lb/ft²)
Leading-edge sweep	26.5°
Trailing edge sweep	5.5°
No of ribs	14 longitudinal
No of spars	7 (I, II, III, IV, IVa, V, Va)
Span (centre section)	8.456m (27ft 8⅞in)
Span (outer sections)	2 x 13.282m (43ft 6⅞in)
Wing chord (outer sections)	6.573m (21ft 6¾in)
Surface covering	flat sheeting
De-icing system	warm-air

Ailerons

Layout	Junkers 'double-wing' (four segments, outer with trim tabs)
Attachment	six-position
Locations	on mid (Tz) and outer (Tf) wings
Surface covering	flat sheeting
Trim displacement	up/down, 10° each way
Inner aileron from normal	up/down, 7° each way
Outer aileron from normal	up 18° 30', down 23°
Inner aileron at take-off & climb	down 20°
Outer aileron at take-off & climb	down 12°
Inner aileron on landing	down 28° (mid-position)
Outer aileron on landing	down 14° 30' (mid-position)
Inner aileron deflection	up 9° 30', down 7° (for landing)
Outer aileron deflection	up 19° 30', down 18° (for landing)

Split flaps

Locations	beneath fuselage and wing centre section
Surface covering	flat sheeting
Operating field (landing)	40° to 58°

Tailplane

Type of construction	all-metal, cantilever
Overall span	12.88m (42ft 3⅛in)
No of ribs	12 longitudinal
No of spars	three
Surface covering	flat sheeting
Variable adjustment	+2° (normal setting) to -3°

Elevator

No of spars	two
Type of support	on three guides each side
Surface covering	flat sheeting (front), corrugated sheeting (rear)
Deflection range	up 40°, down 25°
Trim tab deflection range	up 10°, down 10°

Fins and Rudders

No of spars	three each
Surface covering	flat sheeting (front), corrugated sheeting (rear)
Type of construction	all-metal, cantilever
Attachment	three-point
Range of movement	40° outwards, 30° inwards
Deflection range	10° either way

Undercarriage

Mainwheel dimensions	1450 x 500mm (V1)
	1650 x 600mm (V4)
	1320 x 480mm (V5 to V8)
	1650 x 500mm (Z)
Oleo legs	two EC oleo legs in cast frame
Oleo type	EC or Kronprinz
Mainwheel track	7.320m (24ft 0¼in)
Tailwheel dimensions	780 x 260mm (Z)
Oleo type	EC or Kronprinz
Rotation range	360°
Wheel braking	hydraulic
Positioning by	hydraulic oil (main and tailwheels)
Mainwheel retraction	20 seconds
Mainwheel extension	15 seconds
Extension speed limit	below 200km/h (124mph)

Wireless Equipment

FT-Anlage (W/T)	Lorenz long-wave W/T system
	Telefunken 118N direction-finding (D/F)
	Telefunken 119N bad-weather landing system
Course control	Siemens SAM

Powerplants

Engines (in Ju 90Z-2)	BMW 132H/1
Configuration	nine-cylinder radial
Take-off power	880hp
Starting system	Bosch inertia starter Eclipse ALISGC 24L2
Fuel pump	Junkers Jumo 2016A-2
Fuel feed pump	Ehrich & Graetz ZD 350
Ignition system	Bosch GE 9 BLS 155/156
Aircraft electrical network	29V
Power generators	2 x Bosch LK 1200/24 CL (dc 1200 W)
Batteries	2 x 24V, 75 Ah

Fuel system (according to Handbook)

Wing interim section Tz (V4)	4 x 480 litre tanks with cruising fuel (filled content 4 x 470 litres)
Wing outer sections Tf (V4)	4 x 210 litre tanks with cruising fuel (filled content 4 x 210 litres)
Wing outer sections Tf (V4)	4 x 270 litres take-off fuel (filled content 4 x 270 litres)
Total fuel tank capacity	3,840 litres (3,800 litres actual filling)
Wing interim section (0001/03)	4 x 620 litre tanks for cruising fuel (4 x 470 litres actual filling)

Wing outer sections (0001/03)	4 x 210 litre tanks for cruising fuel (4 x 210 litres actual filling)
Wing outer sections (0001/03)	4 x 270 litres for take-off fuel (4 x 470 litres actual filling)
Total fuel tank capacity	4,400 litres (3,800 litres actual filling)

Lubricant system

Lubricant tanks	4 x 88 litres capacity (4 x 66 litres filling limit)
Coolers	4 retractable coolers of 432cm² (67in²) area
Lubricant type	Intava Rotring or Intava 100 M
Temperature range	motor entry 40°-80° (maximum)

Airscrews

Manufacturer	Junkers, Hamilton licence
Type	Ju HPC-III variable-pitch three-blade metal
Diameter	3.50m (11ft 5¾in)
Pitch range	20°
Airscrew area	4 x 9.62m² (4 x 103.56ft²)

De-icing System

Wing	warm-air de-icing
Inner aileron	Conti de-icer (rubber de-icer, compressed air)
Outer aileron	Conti de-icer
Tailplane and elevator	Conti de-icer
Fins	Conti de-icer

Weight Data

Empty weight	V3: 13,580kg (29,938 lb)
Equipped weight	V3: 15,890kg (35,031 lb)
	V4: 16,450kg (36,266 lb)
	V5: 16,020kg (35,318 lb)
	V6: 18,560kg (40,917 lb)

Fuel weight	V4: 2,490kg (5,489 lb)
Lubricant weight	V4: 180kg (397 lb)
Freight/baggage/mail	V4: 960kg (2,116 lb)
Crew weight	V4: 320kg (705 lb)
Passengers	33 to 38
	V4: 2,640kg (5,820 lb)
Take-off weight (maximum)	V1: 19,000kg (41,887 lb)
	V3: 23,300kg (51,367 lb)
	V4: 23,040kg (50,794 lb) normal
	0002/04: 25,800kg (56,879 lb)

Performance

Maximum permissible speed with	
(a) landing flaps extended	190km/h (118mph)
(b) split flaps extended	160km/h (99mph)
Maximum permissible speed with undercarriage extended	200km/h (124mph)
Max permissible level speed	350km/h (217mph)
Permissible gliding speed	380km/h (236mph)
Maximum speed	V3: 350km/h at 1,100m (217mph at 3,610ft)
Cruising speed	V3: 320km/h at 3,000m (199mph at 9,840ft)
Landing speed	V3:109km/h (68mph)
Times to height	4.2 mins to 1,000m (3,280ft)
	8.7 mins to 2,000m (6,560ft)
	15 mins to 3,000m (9,840ft)
	23.5 mins to 4,000m (13,120ft) for V3
Service ceiling	V3: 4,900m (16,075ft)
Range	V3: 1,540km (957 miles)
Flight duration	V3: 4.8hrs
Take-off run	V3: 600m (1,970ft)
Landing run	V3: 500m (1,640ft)

JUNKERS FLUGZEUG- UND -MOTORENWERKE
AKTIENGESELLSCHAFT   DESSAU

TECHNISCHE DATEN

Nr.: 9053 h
Datum: 8.5.38

FLUGZEUG:
Typ: 4-motoriger Ganzmetall-Tiefdecker   Muster: Ju 90
Verwendung: Verkehr, Fracht   Ausführung: Land

MOTOR:
Fabrikat: Junkers Flugzeug-u.-Motorenwerke   Typ: Jumo 211 C
Bauart: 12 Zyl.flüssigkeitsgekühlter A.G.   Leistung: 4 x 950 PS
Vergaser-Reihenmotor   in 3500 m

LUFTSCHRAUBE:
Typ: Junkers Verstellschraube   Flügelzahl: 3
Baustoff: Metall   Verstellbar: im Fluge verstellbar

GEWICHTE:
Leergewicht . . . . 14200 kg
Gesamtlast . . . . 8850 kg
Fluggewicht . . . . 23050 kg
(Zahlende Nutzlast 3360 kg, bezogen auf 1500 km)

GESCHWINDIGKEITEN:
Max. Geschwindigkeit in Bodennähe . . . . 365 km/h
"   "   in 3500 m Höhe . . . . 400 km/h
Reise-   "   in 3900 m Höhe . max. . . . 363 km/h
"   "   in 3900 m Höhe . wirtsch. . 325 km/h
Lande-   "   . . . . 110 km/h
Anlauf (unter normalen Bedingungen) . . . . m
Auslauf mit/ohne Bremsen . . . . m

HÖHENLEISTUNGEN:
Dienstgipfelhöhe . . . . 7400 m
Theor. Gipfelhöhe . . . . 7900 m
"   "   bei Ausfall eines Motors . . 4900 m
Steigzeit 0—1000 m . . . . 5,1 min
"   0—3000 m . . . . 9,6 min
"   0— m . . . . min

FLUGBEREICH:
Im Reiseflug bei 325 km/h . . ca. 4,5 std. = ca. 1500 km
bei Inhalt der max.Brennstoffbehälter . . . . 3600 ltr.

Flächenbelastung . . . . 125 kg/m²
Leistungsbelastung . . . . 6,07 kg/PS

Bitte wenden!

R.1497/6+7 TK.

JUNKERS FLUGZEUG- UND -MOTORENWERKE
AKTIENGESELLSCHAFT   DESSAU

TECHNISCHE DATEN

Nr.: 9051 L B1.1
Datum: 29.4.38

FLUGZEUG:
Typ: 4-motoriger Ganzmetall-Tiefdecker   Muster: Ju 90
Verwendung: Verkehrs-Großflugzeug   Ausführung: Land, mit einziehbarem Fahrgestell

MOTOR:
Fabrikat: BMW Flugmotorenbau m.b.H.   Typ: BMW 132 Ha
Bauart: untersetzte, luftgekühlte   Leistung: 4 x 830 = 3320 PS
9 Zyl. Sternmotoren   in 1100 m

LUFTSCHRAUBE:
Typ: Junkers-Hamilton-Ju HPC   Flügelzahl: 3
Baustoff: Metall   Verstellbar: im Fluge

GEWICHTE:
Leergewicht . . . . 13520 kg
Gesamtlast . . . . 8740 kg
Fluggewicht . . . . 22260 kg
(Zahlende Nutzlast ~ 2700 kg, bezogen auf 2100 km)

GESCHWINDIGKEITEN:
Max. Geschwindigkeit in Bodennähe . . . . 340 km/h
"   "   in 1100 m Höhe . . . . . 355 km/h
Reise-   "   (max.) 2000 m Höhe (4x 690 PS) . 335 km/h
"   "   in 2500 m Höhe (4x 615 PS) . 325 km/h
Lande-   "   (bei vollem Fluggewicht) . 109 km/h +)
Anlauf (xxxxxxxxxxxxxxxxxxxxx) Startweg bis 20 m . 600 m
Auslauf mit/xxxx Bremsen   Höhe unter   — m

HÖHENLEISTUNGEN:
Dienstgipfelhöhe . . . . 5000 m
Theor. Gipfelhöhe . . . . 5600 m
"   "   bei Ausfall eines Motors 2600 m
Steigzeit 0—1000 m . . . . . . 4 min
"   0—2000 m . . . . . . 9,2 min
"   0—3000 m . . . . . . 15,4 min

FLUGBEREICH: (unter Berücksichtigung des Steigens auf Reisehöhe u.des Gleitflugs)
Im Reiseflug (wirtsch.=315 km/h) 7 std. = ca. 2100 km
bei Inhalt der xxxxx Brennstoffbehälter . . . . 4400 ltr. ++)

Flächenbelastung . . . . 121 kg/m²
Leistungsbelastung . . . . 6,7 kg/PS

+) Landegeschwindigkeit bei 1/3 Betriebsstoff u.
voller Nutzlast: 104 km/h   Bitte wenden!
R.1497/6+7 TK. ++)Die zahlende Nutzlast beträgt bei 1100 k . . . .

Nr.: 9051 L B1.1

JUNKERS FLUGZEUG- UND -MOTORENWERKE
AKTIENGESELLSCHAFT   DESSAU

TECHNISCHE DATEN

Nr.: 9070 H
Datum: 4.5.38

FLUGZEUG:
Typ: 4-motoriger Ganzmetall-Tiefdecker   Muster: Ju 90
Verwendung: Verkehr und Fracht   Ausführung: Land

MOTOR:
Fabrikat: Wright Aeronautical   Typ: Wright Cyclone
Bauart: 9 Zyl.-Sternmotor   Leistung: GR 1820 G 102
4x 910 PS in 1530

LUFTSCHRAUBE:
Typ: Verstell-Luftschrauben   Flügelzahl: 3
Baustoff: Metall   Verstellbar: Vielverstell, ohne Segelstell

GEWICHTE:
Leergewicht . . . . 13800 kg
Gesamtlast . . . . 8990 kg
Fluggewicht . . . . 22790 kg
(Zahlende Nutzlast ~ 2800 kg, bezogen auf 2160 km)

GESCHWINDIGKEITEN:
Max. Geschwindigkeit in Bodennähe . . . . 350 km/h
Max.   Reise-   "   in 1830 m Höhe (Nennhöhe) . 375 km/h
Wirtsch.   "   in 2400 m Höhe . 350 km/h
"   "   in 3000 m Höhe . 325 km/h
Lande-   "   bei vollem Fluggewicht 110 km/h
Anlauf (unter normalen Bedingungen) . . . . . . — m
Auslauf mit/ohne Bremsen . . . . — m

HÖHENLEISTUNGEN:
Dienstgipfelhöhe bei vollem Fluggewicht . . 5800 m
Theor. Gipfelhöhe " . . " . . 6300 m
"   "   bei Ausfall eines Motors " 3800 m
Steigzeit 0—1000 m . . . . . . 3,7 min
"   0—3000 m . . . . . . 12 min
"   0— m . . . . . . min

FLUGBEREICH: einschl. Steig- und Gleitflug
Im Reiseflug in 3000 m b.325 km/h ca.6,6 std. = ca. 2160 km
bei Inhalt der xxxxx Brennstoffbehälter . . . . 4400 ltr. +)

Flächenbelastung . . . . 123,5 kg/m²
Leistungsbelastung . . . . 6,25 kg/PS

+) Die zahlende Nutzlast beträgt bei 1000 km
Reichweite ca. 4600 kg.   Bitte wenden!
R.1497/6+7 TK.

BEMERKUNGEN ZU DEN LEISTUNGSDATEN

Die vorstehenden Werte sind Informationswerte. Garantiedaten werden erst abgegeben, wenn über die Ausrüstung etc. der Maschine vollkommen Klarheit geschaffen ist.

Die Werte gelten für die aufgeführten Motorleistungen, Gewichte, sowie für das Flugzeug ohne zusätzliche Anbauten.

Den Angaben ist die Cina-Atmosphäre zugrunde gelegt.

Motorleistungs- und Betriebsstoff-Verbrauchsangaben nach Mitteilung des Motorenherstellers.

Leergewicht ist das Gewicht des flugfertigen Flugzeuges ohne Besatzung, Betriebsstoff, Nutzlast und Ausstattung.

Höchstgeschwindigkeit ist die Horizontal-Fluggeschwindigkeit bei der angegebenen Motorleistung.

Reisegeschwindigkeit ist die Horizontal-Fluggeschwindigkeit bei etwa 64 % der angegebenen Motorleistung.

Dienstgipfelhöhe ist die Höhe, in der das Flugzeug noch eine Steiggeschwindigkeit von 0,5 m/s hat.

Gipfelhöhe ist die Höhe, in der die Steiggeschwindigkeit gleich Null ist. Sie wird durch geradlinige Verlängerung der Steiggeschwindigkeitskurve in Abhängigkeit von der Höhe ermittelt.

JUNKERS FLUGZEUG- UND -MOTORENWERKE
AKTIENGESELLSCHAFT   DESSAU

Ju 90 Performance with Various Powerplants

The Junkers data sheets, on the opposite page, compiled in 1938, are original documents and provide pertinent information on Ju 90 performance and weights when powered by the Jumo 211, BMW 132 and Wright Cyclone powerplants, and the conditions under which these figures were achieved (fourth data sheet).

The Ju 90Z-3 for South Africa

The accompanying documents refer to the two machines that were destined for South Africa, but which were not delivered. Initially, Werknummer 900002 was flown by the Flugbereitschaft in Berlin and, after a pause for overhaul, was set aside for towing tests with the Messerschmitt Me 321 Gigant glider. In 1942 this aircraft, which was to have towed an Me 321, was rammed on take-off and damaged. In September 1943 it was burned out near Bad Tölz following an unsuccessful emergency landing. Werknummer 900004 also flew initially for the Flugbereitschaft. In April 1940, it too was burned out following a take-off accident at Hamburg-Fulsbüttel.

The two aircraft were ordered under the South African civil registrations ZS-ANG and ZS-ANH, with which they were never adorned. Instead, 900002 was accorded the German civil registration D-APZR, and later the military call-sign KB+LA. The other machine initially sported an unknown civil registration before becoming KB+LB.

Top: **Ju 90Z-3 werknummer 900002.**

Centre left: **A letter from Armstrong Siddeley Motors Ltd to Junkers concerning the possible use of Tiger engines in the SAA-ordered Ju 90.**

Centre right: **A press article from Anhalter Anzeiger concerning the Ju 90s ordered by SAA.**

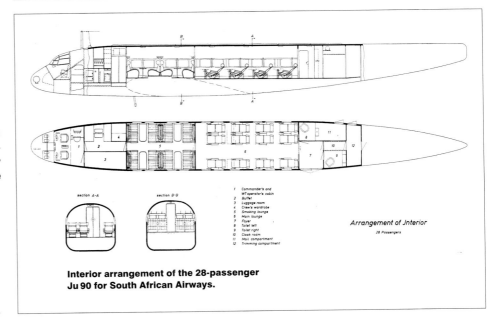

Interior arrangement of the 28-passenger Ju 90 for South African Airways.

Arrangement of Interior
28 Passengers

section A-A   section B-B

1 Commander's and WT operator's cabin
2 Buffet
3 Luggage room
4 Crew's wardrobe
5 Smoking lounge
6 Main lounge
7 Foyer
8 Toilet left
9 Toilet right
10 Cloak room
11 Mail compartment
12 Trimming compartment

Junkers Flug.eug und Motor werk AG Flugzeugbau Stammwerk Dessau	Bearbeitung Kobü-Entwurf Leistungsdat. Da./Hs.	Datum 26.1.40.	Kennzeichnung Nr. 90/217

2.2

Ergebnisse der Flugerprobung der Ju 90
===
002 u.004 (waren für SAA bestimmt)
=========

L... z... Patente
Ein | 2. FEB. 1940

Motoren : 4 x Twin Wasp SC - G
Luftschr.: 4 x 3-flgl. Hamilton Hydromatik-Luftschr. mit Segelstellung.

Beim Flug mit der durch autom. Vergaser bedingten ca. 90 %-Leistung ergaben sich bei einem Fluggewicht von 22,5 t folgende Maximalgeschw.:

v_{max} in Bodennähe bei n = 2550 1/min, p = 35" (N=~4x810 PS) 320 km/h
v_{max} in H = 3000 m " n = 2550 1/min, p = 35" (N=~4x840 PS) 365 "

Die Umrechnung dieser Geschw. auf die in den Motorleistungskurven angegebene "normal rating best power" ergibt:

Größtgeschw. in H = 3660 m bei n = 2550 1/min (N=~4x913 PS) ~ 385 km/h

Reiseflug bei G=22,5 t; Gashebel: Vollgas; Vergasereinstellung: "Reise"
v_{Reise} in Bodennähe bei n=2200 1/min, p=29,5" (~4x610 PS) 285 km/h
v_{Reise} max in H=3750m " n=2200 1/min, p=29,5" (~4x660 PS) 340 "
Kraftstoffverbrauch hierbei (je Motor) 185 l/h

v_{Reise} in Bodennähe bei n=2100 1/min, p=28,5" (~4x575 PS) 275 km/h
v_{Reise} in H=3750m " n=2100 1/min, p=28,5" (~4x600 PS) 330 "
Kraftstoffverbrauch hierbei (je Motor) 172 l/h

v_{Reise} in Bodennähe bei n=2000 1/min, p=28,0" (4x525 PS) 263 km/h
v_{Reise} in H=3750 m " n=2000 1/min, p=28,0" (4x555 PS) 320 "
Kraftstoffverbrauch hierbei (je Motor) 160 l/h

Steiggeschw. m.4 Mot. in H=0 m bei $G_{Abfl.}$=24,4 t (4x800PS,n=2350 1/min) 2,7 m/s
Gipfelhöhe mit 4 Motoren u. $G_{Abfl.}$ = 24,4 t 6600 m
Dienstgipfelhöhe mit 4 Motoren u. $G_{Abfl.}$ = 24,4 t 5900 m

Steiggeschw. m.3 Mot. in H=0 m bei G = 20 t (3x800PS,n=2350 1/min) 2,85 m/s
Dienstgipfelhöhe mit 3 Mot. u. G = 20 t 4600 m

Steiggeschw. m.3 Mot. in H=0 m bei G = 23,5 t (3x800PS,n=2350 1/min) 1,3 m/s
Dienstgipfelhöhe mit 3 Motoren u. G = 23,5 t 3100 m

Dienstgipfelhöhe mit 2 Mot. u. G = 20 t (2x1000PS,n=2600 1/min) 2700 m
Dienstgipfelhöhe " 2 " u. G = 23 t (2x1000PS,n=2600 1/min) 1200 m

---

Junkers Flugzeug-und-Motorenwerke AG Flugzeugbau Stammwerk Dessau	Bearbeitung Kobü-Leistungs- daten Da./Hs.	Datum 20.7.38.	Kennzeichnung

Zur Orientierung!

Leistungen des Landflugzeuges Ju 90
Motoren : 4x Twin Wasp SC - G
Luftschr.: 4x Vielverstellluftschraube mit Segelstellung

Verkehrsflugzeug

allgemeine Daten:
Tragfläche 164 m² Flächenbelastung 128 kg/m²
Spannweite 35,27 m Leistungsbelastung 6,45 kg/PS

Motordaten: Motoren		Twin Wasp SC - G
Motorleistung	PS	4x913
in Nennhöhe	m	3350
bei Drehzahl	1/min	2550/1435
Startleistung (bei 100 Oktan)	PS	4x1215

Gewichte:		
Leergewicht	kg	14225
zusätzl. Ausrüstung	"	2310
Kraftstoff	"	2300
Schmierstoff	t	165
Besatzung	"	520
Nutzlast: 38 Fluggäste	"	3040
Gepäck	"	760
Post	4100 kg	200
Litropa-Zuladung	"	100

Fluggewicht kg 23500
Höchstzul. Startgew.(Startlänge 600m bis 20m Höhe) kg 25800

Leistungen:		
v_{max} in Bodennähe	km/h	340
Reisegeschw. in Nennhöhe (3350 m)	"	390
$v_{R max}$ in H = 4350 m (bei N = 4x610 PS)	km/h	340
v_R wirtsch. in H= 0 m (bei N = 4x520 PS) bei G_m	"	280
v_R wirtsch. in H=4000 m (bei N = 4x560 PS)	"	320
v_{Lande} bei vollem Fluggewicht	km/h	110
v_{Lande} bei 1/3 Betriebsstoff	"	106

Gipfelhöhe	m	7100
Dienstgipfelhöhe	"	6500
Steigzeit 0 ..... 1000 m Höhe	min	4,5
0 ..... 2000 " "	"	9
0 ..... 3000 " "	"	13,5
0 ..... 4000 " "	"	18
Gipfelhöhe b.Ausfall eines Motors b.voller Fluggew. m		5000
Kraftstoffverbr. bei v_R wirtsch.	g/PSh	215
" " " v_R = 320 km/h in H=4000 m	kg/h	481
Flugbereich (einschl.Steig-und Gleitflug) b.v_R = 320 km/h in H = 4000 m	km	1500
Startlänge bis 20 m Höhe	m	ca. 530

Junkers performance results with the two Ju 90s that were intended for SAA.

Junkers data sheet of 20th September 1938 for the Ju 90 powered by four Pratt & Whitney Twin Wasp SC-G engines.

Illustrations below: **Data relating to the Ju 90Z pressurised cabin.**

Ausrüstung der Ju 90 Z mit druckdichtem Fluggastraum

Die Weiterentwicklung der Ju 90 Z sieht als wesentlichste Neuerung die Einführung des druckdichten Fluggastraumes vor. Zum Unterschied von ähnlichen Bestrebungen anderer Flugzeughersteller war dabei der Leitgedanke, den gesamten Kabinenraum schon während des Steigens auf Reisehöhe, beginnend also bereits von ca. 500 m, in Überdruckzustand zu versetzen.

Das frühzeitige Verdichten der Kabinenluft erfüllt den vielfach geäußerten Wunsch der Luftverkehrsgesellschaften, die kurzzeitige Drucksteigerung beim schnellen Landen aus Reisehöhe, soweit wie irgend möglich, auszuschalten. Denn der Wiederanstieg des Raumdruckes auf Bodenatmosphäre ruft bei einer größeren Zahl von Fluggästen, als gewöhnlich angenommen, physische Beeinträchtigungen hervor, die sich nicht immer nur in der einfachen Form eines schnell vorübergehenden Unbehagens äußern, sondern oft auch noch für geraume Zeit auf den Organismus störend nachwirken können.

So beträgt der Druckunterschied schon in 3000 m Höhe gegenüber Bodenatmosphäre 0,31 at. Zur Abhilfe dieses Übelstandes wird in Zukunft bei der Ju 90 Z der Betriebsdruck in der Kabine in der vorgenannten Flughöhe zu 0,16 at über Außenatmosphäre gehalten, sodaß sich nunmehr der Druckunterschied gegenüber Bodenatmosphäre nur zu 0,15 at stellt. Man braucht dann also am Ende der Reiseflugstrecke nur etwas weniger als den halben Druckanstieg zu überwinden. Dieser wird mit Hilfe einer zwischengeschalteten Beruhigungsstufe konstanten Kabinendruckes von 2000 m bis herab auf 500 m Höhe in zwei Teilanstiegen (29 %, 19 %) bewältigt. Damit ergibt sich gleichzeitig der besondere Vorteil, wo die geographischen Verhältnisse es erforderlich machen, von 2000 m ab mit hoher Bahn- und Sinkgeschwindigkeit zur Landung übergehen zu können, ohne daß die Fluggäste durch einen forcierten Druckanstieg irgendwie in Mitleidenschaft gezogen werden.

Aber ein Übergang auf größere Höhen würde den Fluggästen in der in dieser Weise aufgeladenen Kabine den Druckabfall kaum spürbar machen, wenn man bedenkt, daß infolge konstant gehaltener Aufladung der Raumdruck in 4000 m Flughöhe dem Außendruck von 2200 m Höhe entspricht, während er bei 5000 m dem Außendruck von 3000 m äquivalent ist, Höhen also, in welchen der Sauerstoffgehalt der Luft ausreicht, um auf die künstliche Zufuhr durch eine lästige und als wenig hygienisch erkannte, individuelle Sauerstoffanlage noch bedenkenlos verzichten zu können.

Die stetige Förderung ölfreier Ladeluft, die gleichzeitig als Spülluft für die Kabine dient, erfolgt durch Gebläse, die für den Notfall auch auf Reservelieferung bemessen sind. Bei der Errechnung der durchzusetzenden Spülluftmenge war unter der Annahme voll besetzter Kabine einschl. Bedienungspersonal die Erfüllung der Forderung maßgebend, die Fenster, vor Wasserdampfbeschlag zu schützen. Unter Beachtung dieser Gesichtspunkte ist dafür gesorgt, daß der Luftdurchsatz für einen behaglichen Reiseflug voll ausreicht. Der Rückstrom der verbrauchten Kabinenluft erfolgt durch Ventile in die Außenluft, ohne daß die Fluggäste dabei Druckschwankungen

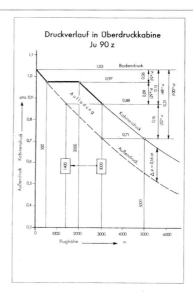

Druckverlauf in Überdruckkabine Ju 90 z

und Geräuschbelästigungen ausgesetzt werden. Die Aufheizung der Luft wurde einer besonderen Durcharbeit unterzogen und die Belüftungsanlage durch die mit Hilfe der Gebläse in einfacher Weise zu erreichende Vorkühlung sämtlicher Räume auf Stand erweitert. Nebenher bleibt die sonst übliche jedem Fluggast gebotene Einzelbelüftung erhalten. Auch der Gütegrad der ausgezeichneten Schallisolation wurde durch den Ausbau der Überdruckkabine in keiner Weise beeinträchtigt.

Der Führerraum wird aus den triftigen Gründen der Gewichtsersparnis und der baulichen Vereinfachung zunächst nicht als Überdruckraum ausgebildet. Dieser schließt hingegen den gesamten zusammenhängenden Komplex des Fluggastraumes, der Kleiderablagen und der Toiletten ein. Der in sich abgedichtete Wirtschaftsraum versieht dabei noch die Aufgabe einer Luftschleuse für den Fall, daß Besatzungsmitglieder vom Führerraum aus während des Fluges die Kabine betreten wollen.

The Ju 90 with High-Altitude Pressurised Cabin

The possibility of equipping the Ju 90Z with a pressurised cabin was considered, but never actually realised. The original documents here show that provision was made for pressurisation to come into operation during the climb, at 500m (1,640ft), the graph illustrating corresponding cabin pressures at up to 5,000m (16,400ft) flying altitude.

The Ju 90S Long-Range Bomber

This Ju 90 variant embodied design features of the Ju 290. At the time it was often described in the foreign press as a Fernbomber (long-range bomber) and, equipped with weapon stands, it could easily have been assumed to be such. The Ju 90 V6 and V7 prototypes, however, concealed the Ju 90S transport equipped with a 'Trapo-Klappe' loading/unloading ramp. The Ju 90S designation, certainly put out to serve a propaganda purpose, lingered for a long time in published literature, and it was authors Karl Kössler and Günter Ott who first correctly placed it in its proper perspective.

The 'Trapo' Ju 90 Transport

The so-called 'Trapo-Klappe' (transport ramp) represented a satisfactory solution to the loading problem, its usefulness being indicated in the accompanying illustrations. This subject will be dealt with in more detail in the *From Original to Model* series on the Ju 290/Ju 390.

Top: **The post-war Stratocruiser, based on the B-29 bomber. An imposing aircraft, it was also the recipient of a pressure cabin.**

Centre: **The Douglas DC-4E Super Mainliner was equipped with a pressurised cabin.**

Bottom left: **The Boeing 307 Stratoliner, which stemmed from the B-17 bomber, likewise had a pressurised cabin.**

Bottom right: **A view of the DC-4E passenger area.**

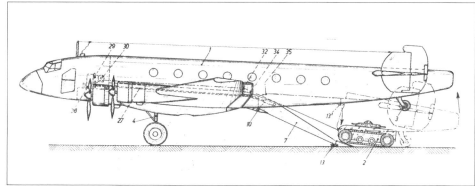

Top: **The Ju 90S embodied several features of the Ju 290. Seen here is the Ju 90 V6 prototype.**

Left: **A tank being loaded via the ramp with the aid of a winch.**

Below left: **The transport ramp could be lowered in flight to release loads or paratroops.**

Below right: **Vehicles could be loaded aboard the aircraft by means of a winch.**

Bottom: **The transition to the Ju 290 is complete. Seen here is the Ju 290 V1 (BD+TX) that originated from the Ju 90 V11.**

Chapter Seven

Airliner

The Ju 90 in Lufthansa Service

Ernst Zindel on Air Travel Development

Ju 90 designer Ernst Zindel commented on air travel development and the resulting requirements with regard to aircraft: 'Based on many years of considerable and multi-faceted experience, particularly with the W 33 and G 24 in freight and passenger service at home and abroad, on land and on water, we decided in 1930 upon the design of a new, modern large-capacity tri-motor aircraft. With its 15-17 passenger seating and crew of three, the Ju 52 became world-renowned and respected. Without being presumptuous, we are able to establish at the present time that this aircraft,

developed in close collaboration with DLH, and which entered airline service in 1932, represented decisive progress in terms of performance, flying characteristics, comfort, safety and reliability, as well as economics. Alongside the well-known DC-2 and DC-3, the Ju 52 is today still the most prolific and best-liked civil aircraft throughout the world, and including its operations as a bomber and transport aircraft, is by far the multi-engined aircraft operated in the greatest numbers worldwide with the greatest of success.

'When we now present as the immediate successor to the tri-motor Ju 52 with its 15-17 passengers, the four-engined Ju 90 with 38-40 passengers as the newest creation of the

Junkers-Flugzeugwerke in the realm of large transport aircraft, you may perhaps well ask how exactly did we arrive at this size and the reason for four instead of three engines?

'The air-traffic related development and technical progress from the thousandfold tested and proven Ju 52 is undoubtedly an extraordinarily large and significant step. The considerations and traffic-related technical requirements that led precisely to the development of the Ju 90 are largely substantiated in the transition from a three- to a four-engined aircraft, namely:

Routes flown by Lufthansa and its associated companies in 1935.

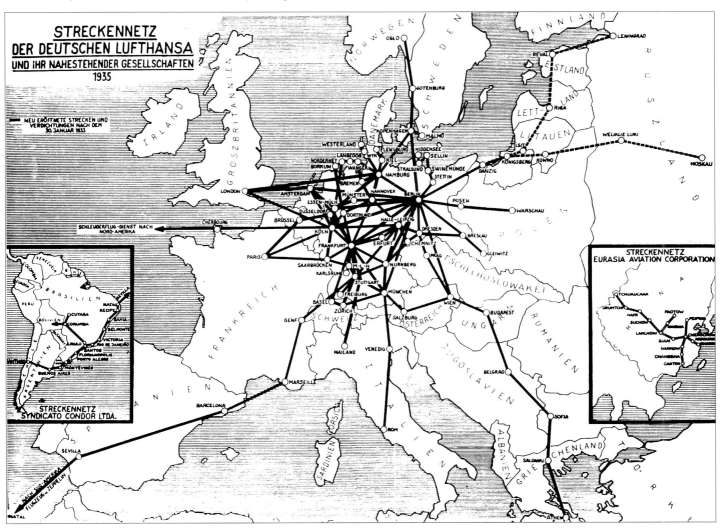

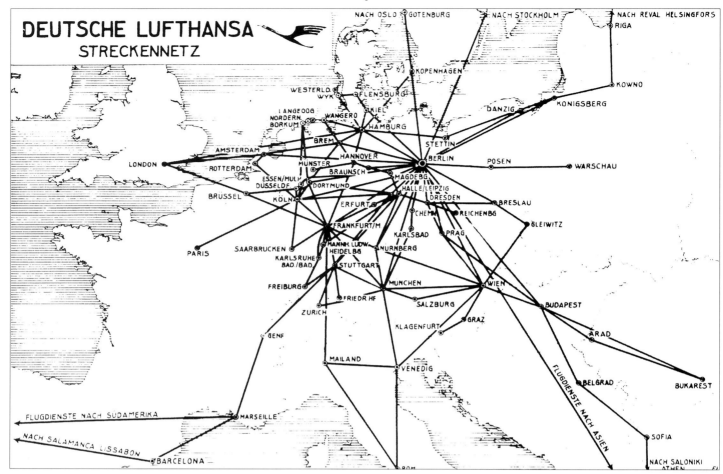

Routes flown by Lufthansa in 1939.

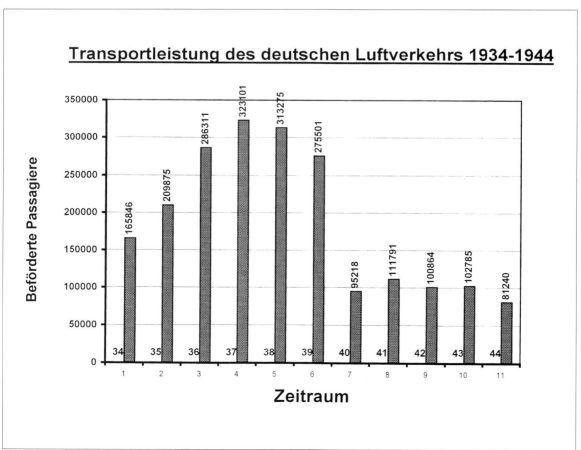

Transportleistung des deutschen Luftverkehrs 1934-1944

Numbers of passengers transported in the period 1934-44 by all German carriers.

1. Use of the Ju 52 especially, as well as Douglas civil airliners, in international air transport in the last five years has brought about an enormous stimulus in the sphere of passenger and freight transportation. This increase in traffic frequency resulted automatically in the necessity for a significant increase in the capacity of the aircraft as a unit.

2. Assuming that over short distances at least, such as on inland routes, that traffic capacity is adequately served by operating several smaller aircraft and thereby attaining a greater concentration of network possibilities – whether this is economically feasible is an open question – there is another reason that compels us to considerably enlarge the aircraft as a unit. On long-distance international air traffic routes that are expected to be flown today partially non-stop, stretches of at least 1,000-2,000km [621-1,242 miles] already come into question, and in the near future distances of at least 3,000km [l,863 miles] have to be reckoned with, that is flying times of between 3 and 8 hours. These present us with the compelling need to do more than was previously necessary to raise passenger comfort. This can, however, only be satisfactorily provided by a considerable enlargement of the passenger cabins, while at the same time achieving this aircraft unit enlargement in an economic fashion.

The fact is that, while it can easily be envisaged that the accepted level of passenger comfort available on an ocean liner cannot be expected on a small coastal steamer with an economically bearable expenditure, a similar situation applies to an aircraft.

'As regards usable crew spaces such as galley, toilets and washrooms, and particularly those for baggage, freight and mailrooms, an increase in range and day-flying facilities will require larger and even additional spaces on board. But even here, the enlargement of the aircraft unit enjoys an advantage over that of the previous normal unit of measurement. The Ju 90, for example, with its 40 passengers, does not need more crew members than the Ju 52 with its 15-17 passengers. Spelled out in figures, each passenger in the Ju 90 has 1.96m³ (69.2ft³) of usable cabin space compared with, for example, the Ju 52 with 1.31m³ (46.3ft³).

'Over and above what these figures exemplify, you will notice the enormous progress made in the layout of the passenger and freight compartments, as well as in the comfort and cosiness of the passengers in the aircraft itself. This is most noticeable, especially on a long-duration flight in the passenger cabins in the Ju 90.

'I trust that with my presentation I have been able to provide you with a picture as to the reasons and considerations that led us to the development of our large four-engined Ju 90

civil airliner, its significant features, facilities, and installations. We also see evidence that very similar thoughts by the overseas manufacturers of the most important civil transport aircraft, particularly in America, have led to similar developments in the sphere of four-engined aircraft.

'We are proud that in Germany, with the Ju 90, we are marching at the forefront of this development of the modern civil aircraft. We hope with the Ju 90 that Germany and the German aviation industry will not only uphold the superb achievement that we have attained in world air travel, but that we shall continue to retain and expand it still further in the future.

'We shall, however, relentlessly strive to push ahead the further development of the Ju 90 that has just entered airline service, in a similar way as we did before with the Ju 52, so that from year to year it will match the needs of air travel and that of the airlines as did the earlier products of the Junkers Flugzeug- und Motorenwerke, and that for many years it shall and will continue to be the most modern and efficient large aircraft.'

Lufthansa in the Years 1937 to 1938

Turning now to the status of Lufthansa in 1937, the company's successful path was accompanied by continually increasing transport figures that were achieved in an ever more tightly knit network of routes. While in 1934 130,578 passengers (44,535,932 passenger-km) with 211,210kg (465,634 lb) of baggage, 1,270,284kg (2,800,468 lb) of freight and 703,659kg (1,551,287 lb) of mail were transported, this increased in 1937 to 277,347 passengers (102,700,917 passenger-km), 394,843kg (870,471 lb) of baggage, 1,313,888kg (2,896,597 lb) of freight and 3,349,132kg (7,383,496 lb) of mail. In the following year, the corresponding Lufthansa report showed a slight decrease in figures – passenger numbers fell to a total of 254,716 – except in the airmail category, which increased to 5,288,531kg (11,659,095 lb).

Even in 1937 the Ju 52 formed the backbone of the Lufthansa fleet. However, the easy-going 'Tante Ju' and other aircraft types that appeared in following years were scheduled to receive significant support from the four-engined Fw 200 and Ju 90 airliners. We shall now take a look at the composition of the Lufthansa fleet in 1938, the largest proportion of which consisted of Junkers aircraft, as the following list shows:

1	Blohm und Voss Ha 139	4	Junkers F 24
2	Dornier Do 18	1	Junkers W 33
2	Dornier 10-tonne Wal	7	Junkers W 34
4	Focke-Wulf Fw 58	1	Junkers G 38
2	Focke-Wulf Fw 200	3	Junkers Ju 46
9	Heinkel He 111	73	Junkers Ju 52*
1	Heinkel He 116	12	Junkers Ju 86
4	Junkers F 13*	17	Junkers Ju 160

* Various aircraft were employed in South America

The fleet list comprises 151 aircraft, but because of the loss of the *Preussen* does not contain a Ju 90. According to Lufthansa planning, during the 1939/40 period five Ju 90A aircraft and five Ju 90Bs with higher-performance powerplants were to have been added from the autumn of 1940. In 1941, more precisely up to the end of March, planning called for a further 20 examples of the Fw 200 Condor. In 1937 the orders placed with aircraft and aero-engine firms had a total value of RM 11,500,000, which increased in the following year to RM 24,000,000. The actual number of Ju 90s procured is shown in the table below.

During the summer of 1939 until the outbreak of war, the Ju 90 flew mainly on the following routes:

- 90 x Berlin-Frankfurt-Munich-Vienna
- 20 x Berlin-Königsberg
- 12 x Berlin-Amsterdam-London

Flying operations came to a complete standstill on 30th August 1939.

Junkers Ju 90 in Lufthansa Service

Werknummer	Registration	Lufthansa name	Year Built	To Lufthansa
4914	D-AIVI	*Preussen*	1937	1938
4915	D-AURE	*Bayern*	1938	1938
4916	D-ADLH	*Schwabenland/Sachsen*	1938	1940
900001	D-ABDG	*Württemberg*	1939	1939
900003	D-ADF J	*Baden*	1939	1939
900005	D-AEDS	*Preussen*	1939	1939
900006	D-ASND	*Mecklenburg*	1939	1939
900007	D-AFHG	*Oldenburg*	1939	1939
900008	D-ATDC	*Hessen*	1939	1940
900009	D-AJHB	*Thüringen*	1939	1940
900010	D-AVMF	*Brandenburg*	1940	1940

Flugkapitän Blankenburg

Das Unglück beim Start in Bathurst

Trauer um die elf deutschen Pioniere der Luft – Der Absturz der viermotorigen „Preußen"

Zu dem bereits kurz gemeldeten Unfall eines deutschen Flugzeuges am Sonnabendnachmittag auf dem Flugplatz in Bathurst (Westafrika) wird ergänzend berichtet:

Von den 15 Insassen ist die aus Flugkapitän Untucht, Flugkapitän Blankenburg, Oberfunkermaschinist Gillwald, Flugzeugfunker Sager und Flugmaschinist Cardong bestehende Besatzung, ferner vom Reichsluftfahrtministerium Fliegerstabsingenieur Schwendler und die für navigatorische Zwecke eingesetzten Handelskapitäne Andrae, Benthien und Sutter und vom Motorenwerk die beiden Monteure Pfäfflin und Hasenmüller ums Leben gekommen, während Diplomingenieur Schinzinger, Diplomingenieur Hansen und Ingenieur Thieme leicht und Diplomingenieur Feßler schwer verletzt wurden. Die deutsche Unfall-Untersuchungskommission befindet sich auf dem Wege nach Bathurst.

Das Junkers-Flugzeug, dessen Besatzung von dem Unglück betroffen wurde, war eine viermotorige Ju 90. Die Maschine, die den Namen „Preußen" trug, war am Mittwoch in Dessau aufgestiegen um im Rahmen der Erprobungsflüge, die die Deutsche Lufthansa in aller Welt vornehmen läßt, nach Afrika zu fliegen. Nach Zwischen-

Kartendienst des BLA

landungen in Marseille und Las Palmas wurde die Reise nach der afrikanischen Küste fortgesetzt. Am Sonnabendnachmittag wurde Bathurst, der Startort der Postflieger nach Südamerika, erreicht, und nach kurzem Aufenthalt stieg die

Maschine zu einem Probe- und Meßflug auf. Da das Flugzeug nach normalem Start nicht genügend Höhe gewann, berührte es am Rande des Flugplatzes eine Palme und stürzte zu Boden.

Die Aufgabe der Besatzung war es, die klimatischen Bedingungen im transkontinentalen Verkehr zu prüfen, die starken und schnellen Schwankungen zwischen gemäßigten und tropischen Breiten festzustellen und damit den Einsatz von Großflugzeugen im Verkehr zwischen den Erdteilen vorzubereiten. Zu diesem Zwecke hatte man eine ganze Reihe von Verbesserungen an dem Flugzeug angebracht. Erstmalig war z. B. eine Enteisungsanlage eingebaut, denn die Vereisung der Tragflächen ist ein gefährlicher Feind eines sicheren Flugverkehrs. Es war vorgesehen, daß die Maschine von Dakar oder Bathurst aus ausgiebige Versuchsflüge über die innerafrikanischen Wüsten machen sollte. Dabei wollte man das Verhalten der Maschine in heißen Gegenden studieren. Die Maschine besaß vier BMW-132-Motoren. Es wurde also mit Benzin, nicht mit Rohöl geflogen.

Die Führung des Flugzeuges hatte man Männern anvertraut, die in Deutschland und aller Welt als Pioniere des Flugwesens einen Namen haben. An erster Stelle wurde die Maschine von Flugkapitän Robert Untucht geführt, der mit Frhr. v. Gablenz von der Lufthansa das Pamir-Plateau bezwang und mit diesem Flug über das „Dach der Welt" eine ganz besondere Leistung vollbracht hatte. Zweiter Pilot war Flugkapitän Joachim Blankenburg, der einzige Flieger, der mehr als hundert Ozeanflüge zurückgelegt hat. Mit Untucht und Blankenburg gehörte Diplomingenieur Schinzinger zur Besatzung, der bisher alle Ozeanüberquerungen der Junkers-Werke technisch vorbereitet hat. Seine Aufgabe war es, bei dem Afrikaflug die Messungen des Brennstoff- und Ölverbrauchs vorzunehmen und die Maschinentemperaturen in den Tropen zu beobachten. Die technische Gesamtleistung lag in den Händen von Diplomingenieur Feßler.

*

Mit tiefer Erschütterung vernehmen wir die schmerzliche Kunde von der Vernichtung des deutschen Großflugzeugs, das 4200 Kilometer von der Heimat entfernt auf dem Boden Afrikas verunglückte. In Trauer beugt sich ganz Deutschland über das tragische Schicksal, das es seiner Pio...

Disaster: The Bathurst Catastrophe

The introductory phase of the Ju 90 was quickly overshadowed by a catastrophe suffered by Werknummer 4914, D-AIVI, christened *Preussen*.

Under the headline 'Accident at Take-Off in Bathurst' and accompanied by photographs of Flugkapitän Robert Untucht and co-pilot Flugkapitän Joachim Blankenburg, the *Berliner Lokalanzeiger* newspaper described the tragic accident, which, despite fears, did not damage the image of the Ju 90. It was as a result of political events that the heyday of Lufthansa, and with it the Ju 90, came to an abrupt end. In the course of 1939, in accordance with agree-

A newspaper article in the *Berliner Lokalanzeiger* of 28th November 1938 regarding the take-off accident suffered by Lufthansa's Ju 90 *Preussen* at Bathurst, Gambia.

ments, Lufthansa gave up a significant portion of its fleet to TG 172 for military use, as well as to the Luftwaffe's training organisation, to which four further organisations were added, strengthened by the addition of four aircraft from the Lufthansa aircraft park. TG 172 took over a total of 65 machines of various types – one Fw 200, one G 38, one He 111, 59 Ju 52s and three Ju 90s – of which only six had been returned to Lufthansa by the end of 1939. The training units received 43 aircraft, among them ten Ju 86s and eight Ju 160s.

Life Histories: Ju 90s in Lufthansa Service and their Locations

Following the introductory phase of the Ju 90 and the accident at Bathurst, we now look at significant details in the individual histories of each Ju 90 belonging to the Lufthansa fleet.

Werknummer 4914, D-AIVI *Preussen*

Lufthansa took over this aircraft on 26th May 1938, with a testing phase extending until the end of June. In the course of 104 flying hours, almost all of the German civil airports had been covered. This test phase ended on 18th July 1938, and, as already related, *Preussen* was lost in the take-off disaster at Bathurst.

Werknummer 4915, D-AURE *Bayern*

Bayern joined the Lufthansa fleet in July 1938. After network testing lasting six weeks, an Me 109 collided with it on 11th August while taking off, damaging the port wing of the Ju 90. Repairs kept *Bayern* grounded until 2nd September. Thereafter, its travels on a demonstration tour took it through Scandinavia. The final destination was Dessau, where further works trials were carried out.

During the Sudeten crisis, D-AURE was on the inventory of TG 172, but from 12th October 1938 was returned to airline service. From 13th November it was operated on the Berlin-Vienna route, but as of 19th December it was removed and ferried over to Dessau. Despite its comparatively short period of use, this aircraft alone flew 0.4% of the entire Lufthansa transportation volume during 1938. This is all the more remarkable as it covered no less than 62,572km (38,882 miles) during that short space of time.

During the war, in particular during Operation *Weserübung* – the occupation of Denmark and Norway – *Bayern* participated as a military transport with 4./KGr z.b.V.107. In July 1940 it returned to Lufthansa, where it was assigned to the Spanish route. In the course of its further employment, D-AURE served as transport for the German-French Weapons Ceasefire Commission. From April 1943 its use on the Spanish route has been documented. On one of these Spanish flights, during an interim stop at Stuttgart on 9th August 1944, *Bayern* met an unexpected end when it became the victim of American low-flying aircraft. Although the aircraft was burned out, there were fortunately no human casualties.

Its namesake was D-AITR *Bayern*, a Ju 290, part of a little-known chapter in the history of Lufthansa, which now also had the Ju 290 on its inventory. The machines were provided with camouflage and bore the individual Lufthansa name and airline insignia in the fuselage nose region, details that likewise applied to the Ju 290 D-AITQ *Preussen*. Both aircraft will be covered more extensively in the 'From Original to Model' series.

Werknummer 4916, D-ADLH
Schwabenland

This aircraft, the Ju 90 V4, was initially named *Schwabenland*, later becoming *Sachsen*. From 12th January 1940 it was returned to service by Lufthansa and until 23rd February that year flew the Rangsdorf-Danzig-Königsberg route. This machine was also used as a transport during Operation *Weserübung*. It subsequently returned to Lufthansa airline service, but on 21st November 1940 it was damaged in an accident at Vienna. It was not until the beginning of May 1941 that the aircraft again became available on Lufthansa route K 22, which it flew until around mid-July 1941, after which the Ju 90 returned to military duties, bearing the call-sign KH+XA. In connection with its conversion to the Jumo 211F powerplant, the aircraft was ferried that same month to the Weser Flugzeugbau in Lemwerder, where conversion work lasted until October 1942. From November 1942 until the end of March 1943 the aircraft was used by the Luftverkehrsgruppe (Air Transport Group) Berlin, being taken over thereafter by the LTS 290 and Transport-fliegerstaffel 5. In August 1944 it moved once again to TG 4. Located in northern Germany at the end of the war, it was captured there by British troops and later scrapped.

Werknummer 900001, D-ABDG
Württemberg

Württemberg was added to the Lufthansa aircraft fleet on 4th May 1939, and as the first of the small-scale series production aircraft, was extensively tested like its predecessor. The test phase ended on 16th May with its return flight to Dessau. On 31st May *Württemberg* accomplished its first Lufthansa route flight. The following year, it also took part in Operation *Weserübung*, and was further employed at the Luftwaffe E-Stelle Tarnewitz on weapons and turret tests from 30th April 1941 almost until the end of the war.

In civil use it at first bore the civil marking D-ABDG, but from September 1942 this was replaced by the call-sign GF+GB. Captured by British troops in May 1945, it was scrapped on an unknown date.

Werknummer 900003, D-ADFJ *Baden*

Upon its acceptance by Lufthansa on 20th May 1939, the aircraft began to fly on the Lufthansa network as early as the 24th. In 1940 *Baden* also played its part in Operation *Weserübung*. Far more spectacular was its participation in the Frachtsonderdienst Wien (Freight Special Service – Vienna), for which purpose it was set aside on 5th July 1940. In the course of this undertaking, however, it suffered minor damage, for example on 9th July near Udine, where the clearly civilian *Baden* was mistakenly identified by an Italian fighter pilot as a British reconnaissance aircraft and fired upon, resulting in an unplanned landing at Aviano. Bearing Iraqi

insignia, in June 1941 *Baden* took part in the unsuccessful Iraq operation. Towards the end of that month it again appeared with its original markings and was used on the Spanish route. Almost two years later, with LTS 290 in May 1943, it became the victim of enemy bombing in Italy.

Werknummer 900005, D-AEDS *Preussen*

This aircraft, one of the small-scale production series, was also christened *Preussen*. It joined the Lufthansa fleet on 21st July 1939 and during the same month flew the Berlin-Vienna route. After a short period of operation, defects in the heating system were experienced, and in order to have them resolved, the aircraft remained at Junkers in Dessau until 29th September. After that, it did not return to routine service, since from 15th April 1940 it was assigned to special operations, with Spain as its destination. This involved its use on the so-called Frachtsonderdienst Wien (Special Freight Service – Vienna) in which rare metals such as tungsten and tin were to be transported to Germany; the flight route led from Vienna over Viterbo (Italy) to Barcelona. Between 21st April and 13th July 1940, the Lufthansa Ju 90s D-ADLH, D-ABDG, D-ADFJ and D-AURE followed. For these missions the machines were appropriately modified: the entire internal luxury, in the shape of the cabin fittings, galley and toilets, disappeared to be replaced by more conservative requirements. Of significant importance now was the increase in fuel capacity to 5,135 litres. Plywood planks and skirting boards ran along the cabin flooring, so that three tonnes of sacks containing ore could be firmly secured against the fear of sliding.

The occupation of France entailed shorter and less dangerous flights, then from 16th July 1940 the Kurierdienst Spanien (Courier Service – Spain) replaced the former Frachtsonderdienst Wien. The starting point was now Stuttgart, the route then going via Lyon to Barcelona, a distance of less than two-thirds of the original route. A further change took place on 20th August 1940, when this service gave way to the Lufthansa route K 22, operated until the end of the war. The route now started from Berlin via Stuttgart, Lyon, Marseilles and Barcelona to Madrid. From October the route was extended to Lisbon, Portugal. Flown on a daily basis, the K 22 route represented one of the most important Lufthansa connections until the end of the war.

In order to investigate the causes of the crash of the *Brandenburg*, D-AEDS was ordered to München-Oberwiesenfeld for icing trials. It was from here that from 9th December 1940 the icing-up tendency of the elevator, as well as that of the rudder balance, was to be studied, parallel to the investigations at the AVA Göttingen.

Preussen took part in the Iraq operation in May 1941, after which it was again in Lufthansa service the following month on the Spanish

route. It is also known that the aircraft was assigned to LTS 290 Transportfliegerstaffel 5 and 11./TG 4, the latter during the period April 1943 to August 1944. When the war ended in May 1945, northern Germany was occupied by British troops, and *Preussen* was among the numerous captured aircraft. As no further use was made of it, it too was scrapped on an unknown date.

Werknummer 900006, D-ASND
Mecklenburg

This aircraft joined the Lufthansa aircraft park on 28th June 1939, and as soon as 1st August was placed on route service. From 24th July 1940 *Mecklenburg* was assigned to the K 22 (Berlin-Madrid) route. In February 1942 it was transferred to the Luftverkehrs-gruppe (Air Traffic Group) Berlin, and from May 1943 was operated by LTS 290. Little is known regarding its whereabouts. It has been reported that *Mecklenburg* was probably destroyed on the ground by gunfire in November 1943.

Werknummer 900007, D-AFHG *Oldenburg*

Oldenburg joined the Lufthansa fleet on 22nd December 1939. It was the last machine (according to the contract of 4th December 1938) to be purchased at the original price of RM 600,000,and the ferry flight from Dessau took place on 27th December 1939. During a landing in Vienna on 18th June 1940, as had previously happened to *Hessen*, *Oldenburg* suffered damage due to undercarriage collapse, the necessary repairs lasting until September. On 26th May 1941 it again suffered damage in a belly landing, caused by failure due to vibration in the starboard fin. It was cleared for flight again on 9th July. It is known that during the period December 1942 to November 1943 *Oldenburg* was used by the Luftverkehrs-gruppe Berlin. In the winter of 1942/43 it survived an unknown number of provisions flights to the Eastern Front, but met its end with LTS 290 on 23rd July 1943 through enemy fire and the resulting emergency ditching at Bastia, Corsica. German flak also made its contribution.

Werknummer 900008, D-ATDC *Hessen*

Hessen completed its transfer flight from Dessau to its future owner on 2nd March 1940. Two months later, on 6th May, it suffered minor damage to the wing, caused by a botched landing in Danzig following undercarriage failure, resulting in damage to the port outer and interim wing sections. It became available for use again only in October 1940, but soon suffered yet more damage, on 30th April 1941, when, during a landing approach in gusty wind conditions, it struck a wall and, on setting down on the runway, the starboard undercarriage broke. On 24th July *Hessen* became operational once more, but met its fate during a mission on the Eastern Front, when an undercarriage

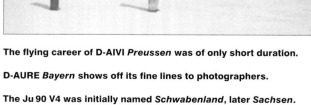

The flying career of **D-AIVI** *Preussen* was of only short duration.

D-AURE *Bayern* shows off its fine lines to photographers.

The Ju 90 V4 was initially named *Schwabenland*, later *Sachsen*.

D-ABDG *Württemberg*, the first of the small-scale production series.

D-ADFJ *Baden* was operated by Lufthansa from 1939 to 1943.

Seen here is the second *Preussen*, Werknummer 900005, which took the place of the earlier machine that crashed in Bathurst.

A frontal view of **D-ASND** *Mecklenburg*, delivered in July 1939.

failure was again responsible. Due to a lack of spare parts, as well as the fact that Kharkov had to be evacuated, the aircraft was no longer able to be repaired, and on 30th January 1943 it was blown up in Kharkov.

Werknummer 900009, D-AJHB *Thüringen*
This aircraft, manufactured in 1939, joined the Lufthansa fleet in 1940. In the period that followed it was another aircraft used on the legendary K22 route. Photographs show it with a grey upper coat (most probably RLM 02) and silver-coloured undersides. In May 1941 *Thüringen* also took part in the so-called Iraq operation. All three of the aircraft used there reverted to their original markings in June. After the Iraq episode, it was again employed on the Spanish route, and its use by LTS 290 in 1943 has also been mentioned. *Thüringen* fulfilled its final tasks during the period January to August 1944 at the Luftwaffe E-Stelle Tarnewitz on weapons and turret trials, where it was reportedly destroyed in August 1944, but the circumstances in relation to this are not known.

Werknummer 900010, D-AVMF *Brandenburg*
This aircraft joined the Lufthansa fleet in May 1940 and had only a short flying life. Following its use on several routes, it crashed near Brauna, a village near Kamenz in Saxony, due to icing during a flight on the Berlin-Prague-Vienna route, with the loss of 29 lives. Because of its short period of operation, *Brandenburg* was the only Ju90 used exclusively by Lufthansa. Unfortunately, only a few photographs exist of this aircraft.

Top left: **D-AFHG *Oldenburg* takes aboard its paying passengers.**

Top right: **D-AHJB *Thüringen* entered the Lufthansa fleet in 1940.**

Above left: **The eighth series-production aircraft was given the Lufthansa name *Hessen*.**

Above right: **Seen here is a partial port-side view of D-AVMF *Brandenburg*.**

Right: **D-AVMF *Brandenburg* was Werknummer 900010 and was the last Ju90 to enter the Lufthansa fleet. As no original photograph is available, pictured here is a scale model.**

Chapter Eight

Modelling the Ju 90

To conclude the technical and historical review of the Ju 90, we shall now concern ourselves with information relevant to the modelmaker.

Ralf Schlüter, an experienced modelmaker, has provided a construction report in words and photographs of the creation of a Ju 90 vacu-model – a type of modelling that requires more skill than a conventional pressure die-cast kit. The entire internal fittings of the model, for example, are all 'hand-made'. Unfortunately, the Ju 90 or Ju 290 is available exclusively in vacu-form. For the inexperienced, this type of model building will possibly present some problems, although they are not insurmountable. As you can imagine, it needs a measure of 'glue and patience'. The author wishes the modelmaking fraternity among his readers much fun and success in making the Ju 90!

The Kit

The only known construction kit is an old *Airmodell* vacuum kit from the 1970s, which is regrettably no longer available, but which for the interested modeller may well be obtainable on the second-hand market. As with all *Airmodell* vacuum kits, this one offers a good structural basis for making all civil and military-use Ju 90 prototypes and small-scale series production aircraft powered by the BMW 132 engine.

Construction

First of all, it must be decided what is to be built. My choice was for Werknummer 900010, D-AVMF *Brandenburg* – the only Ju 90 that was operated exclusively in Lufthansa service from May 1940 until its crash on 8th November 1940. It was fitted out as a standard 40-seater airliner.

We begin with the fuselage parts. The separation from the template and the forming of the profiles is standard vacuum practice. Window separation follows at the points indicated; bore four holes at the extreme corners, cut along the intermediate spaces, then finish off with a file (8.7 x 5.3mm with spacings of 12 and 2mm filed precisely). Assistance can be obtained here with an aluminium block as a home-made hole-gauge with hand-grip, fashioned to the size of the window measurements with a strip of sticky-tape fixed along the top of the windows as support. The hole-gauge then serves as a stencil to withdraw the windows. The small windows and doors are made to open according to the plans.

We turn now to the internal fittings. In the original, the flooring was continuous except in two places: behind the cockpit, ahead of the forward baggage compartment to the entrance at the left, was a step leading down to the folding position of the forward door, and in the forward passenger cabin, above the wing, there was a 2mm step up then down again (above the largest wing thickness). Since these steps remain hidden by the seats, I dispensed with them. Glue the frames and partition walls on to the continuous floor; these construction groups form a stabilising basis for the fuselage. Now add the details according to the photographs and sketches.

Make the pilots' seats from flat parts, with drawn plastic 'tree-branches'. Cut out the instrument dashboard from a flat sheet and use a computer impression to represent the instruments. Form the central control console as a sandwich-type of construction, resulting in a control console with ten slits for the operating levers. Cut out the levers from drawn plastic, heat them briefly over a flame into a drop shape and, with smooth pliers, press them flat to represent the disc-shaped handgrips. Form the central console out of vertically mounted plates, cut out the rotatable knobs from drawn plastic (of thicker diameter) and glue vertically positioned narrow plastic strips to it. Form the trim wheels from discs of larger diameter, glue them to short pieces of drawn plastic and glue all the parts together as shown in the illustration. Using the same method, complete the remaining small parts and attach as illustrated.

In the passenger cabins I used centimetre-length pieces for the seats, with long strips cut out from plastic remainders for the seats, backs and side surfaces. Glue the seat-backs and other surfaces to form a right angle, then the head-rest strips at head-level, then, at an angle, glue on the back-rest. File off these seating strips to represent twin-seats. For the peripheral attachments (arm-rests and head-rests), use a stack of excess rectangular pieces. Press these together at top and bottom, file them to shape and glue them to the seats. Now fix the twin-seats to the transverse frames, with the blocks of four seats placed in between.

As regards colours, the cockpit is in light grey, with black instrument and console surfaces, black seats and back-rests, and white seat-belts (out of aluminium strips). The passenger cabins have blue-grey seats, light grey flooring and beige walls.

When all this has been completed, join together the fuselage shells loosely over the internal fittings, without using pressure. Help can be gained here along the joint by gluing alternate strips 15mm long and 8mm wide to represent the ventilation openings along the upper cabin decking.

After the fuselage has become a firm unit, add the frames for the tailplane and wing, smooth the glue joints, and add the strip with the seven ventilation exhaust-ports over two-thirds of the fuselage length. With the fuselage transverse frames, pay careful attention to the constant diameter of the fuselage in relation to the pre-formed strakes at the wing and fin ends. I sealed the fuselage join over a length of 2cm only after the wing and fin was glued on.

The most delicate part on the fuselage is the cockpit transparency. This acetate component of the kit is usable, having been made to fit exactly, and can serve as a template when filing down the two fuselage shells to the correct diameter prior to joining them. As supports for the cabin roof, glue supporting strips to the edges of the cockpit. If these have been well matched, only a small amount of filler material will be necessary. Thanks to the wide sliding frames on the cockpit, a good finish at these transition points is possible.

Wing

As is normal with vacu-kits, all parts have to cut out and smoothed down. Join the outer wing halves together and smoothen off – in particular, file the root rib. At this location, cut out a window for the spar attachment. Glue the spar to a piece of left-over sheet and file to form a box shape. This is then inserted into the root rib and matched to height. File slits into the wing trailing edge at the designated points and glue on over-dimensioned L-shaped hinge supports. Shape these into their final form with knife and sandpaper.

The wing centre section is still in two parts at this stage. Cut out a rectangular window in the upper portion for insertion of the continuous cabin flooring. Now form the box-shaped central spar and fit it into this upper component, likewise cutting out the undercarriage shafts from above into the upper portion. After that, attach the underside of the wing centre section and, when this is done, file the end ribs. Now glue the outer wing portions to the centre section, guided by the spars. If the end ribs have been filed well, no filler will be necessary at these locations. On the original, the transition from the wing centre section to the outer wings had only a small step, formed by the interim screw-on skin strip.

Empennage

When joining the tailplane halves, use a stiffening strip; in this case a strip of metal sheet would be useful for tailplane adjustment at a later stage. As was done with the wing, file appropriate cut-outs for the tailplane hinges. This time, attach the over-large L-shaped hinge supports from above and form to shape. Fix firmly and open the channels for insertion of the push-rods to the tailplane trailing edge. Precisely at this position, glue a roughly 1mm thick round mast beneath the elevator. This serves as a main support for the elevator to the tailplane. The same procedure is applied for the fins and rudders. Now glue the tailplane to the preset frames in the fuselage. If necessary, adjust to the fuselage width, but do not attempt to adjust by filing the fuselage struts, as their strength is minimal!

Control Surfaces and Airframe Mounting

For the attachment of the ailerons and flaps to the wing, mark the hinge positions and cut out rectangular openings from above. Prior to attachment at an even distance, pay attention to the lower ends of the hinges, then glue on the ailerons and flaps from beneath. Fit the elevator thorn into the push-rod channel and push them along the hinges; the same applies for the rudders.

The Powerplants

Separate all the cowling parts from the engine nacelles and build them separately. Fashion the powerplants from the spare-parts box, or mould them yourself. For the propellers, one can either cannibalise them from the *Italeri* Ju 86E or use these as templates for scratch-built examples. Attach details such as the wing de-icing intake on top the engine, as well as the heating intake on the exhaust port. Make the oil cooler significantly larger than on the plan. Fix the outer nacelles to the outer wing sections. For mounting the engines, the firewalls and equipment support coverings are helpful. Visually very attractive is cutting out and filing thin the radiator flaps.

The Undercarriage

The main undercarriage legs are made from plastic tubes inserted into each other, obtainable from a model kit dealer. The two main legs consist of an x-shaped frame of 0.8mm plastic. Make the forward and rear struts as retractable cylinders. Of assistance here are the built-in attachment lugs. The wheels provided in the kit are awful and need to be modified. Put the wheels together and, after the glue has dried thoroughly, cut out the wheel rims. The new rims are now built up from plastic tubing. The rims are simply made from tubing cut to slightly greater than tyre thickness. With the appropriate internal diameter, the brake-wheel is then filed off and fitted with two enclosing discs. A wheelcap of small diameter provides the correct visual appearance. The brake-wheel is now pushed into the wheel rim and the axle bored through. At the lower end of the undercarriage leg, bore the axle attachment points and, after attaching the brake cables, push the axle pinions through the undercarriage and wheel components. Then insert the whole into the undercarriage shaft. Here, the previously bored spar is an enormous help. Complete the undercarriage doors, together with internal structures, and attach them.

Markings

On some photographs the Ju 90 appears as though its outer skin is of polished aluminium. I decided, however, to adopt the more probable variation consisting of aluminium-colour RLM 01. The best result for a high-gloss finish is possible with *Revell* 90, although I used the more matt 66 version. If *Humbrol* metallic colours are used, it should be remembered that these cannot be lacquered over. Here, the *Revell* colours are more robust, even if the end result has a slightly rougher appearance. Hence, first the aluminium colour, then clear lacquer, then the black letter markings. I did the lacquering before final assembly, since at that stage the stencils are easier to place in position. Incidentally, the latter were cut from typing paper and made durable with non-permanent spray-on glue. One warning: before fixing on to the model, use up the glue on other surfaces so as to avoid smearing. If the model is cleanly worked upon and sealed with clear lacquer, the coating does not suffer during the course of further attention. Following final assembly, only the skinning around the glued spots needs to be lacquered again.

A final word now concerning the external surface structure. The vacu materials here are very rough and need extensive smoothing with sandpaper, after which the joints can be fashioned. I make overlapping joints visible by masking with tape and spraying over with bright grey matt lacquer on the glued edges. The tape is then removed before the colours are dry, to avoid breakage at the joints. When these positions are clearly indicated prior to final assembly of the various components, it makes the work much easier.

The corrugated sheeting visible on the end-plate rudders and in the cockpit is fashioned from aluminium foil, cut to shape, corrugated, and attached with clear lacquer.

Summary

The Ju 90 from *Airmodell* offers a solid vacu basis for making a good Ju 90 model without the necessity to correct configuration errors by the kit manufacturer. However, much luck is needed at the present time to come across such a kit. It would be a fine thing if the largest of our model kit manufacturers would show compassion and include the Ju 90 in their offerings once more! The completed aircraft is, in any case, an eye-opener and a fascinating scale model.

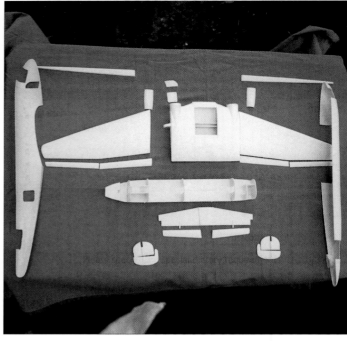

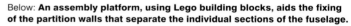

Top left: **The parts of the Ju 90 vacu kit that first have to be cut out. The single-engined Ju 160 parts, laid out at the bottom right, enable a size comparison to be made.**

Top right: **An overview of the parts that have already received the necessary attention in the Ju 90 vacu kit.**

Left: **The same parts provisionally assembled for this plan view.**

Below: **An assembly platform, using Lego building blocks, aids the fixing of the partition walls that separate the individual sections of the fuselage.**

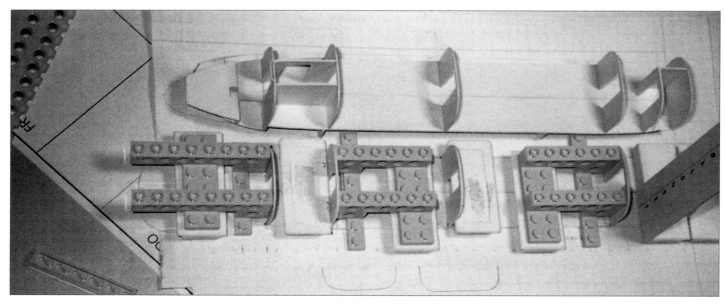

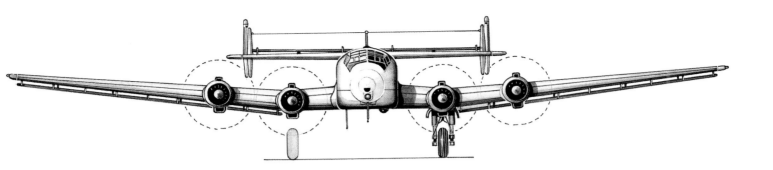

Head-on view of the Ju 90 V3, Werknummer 4915.

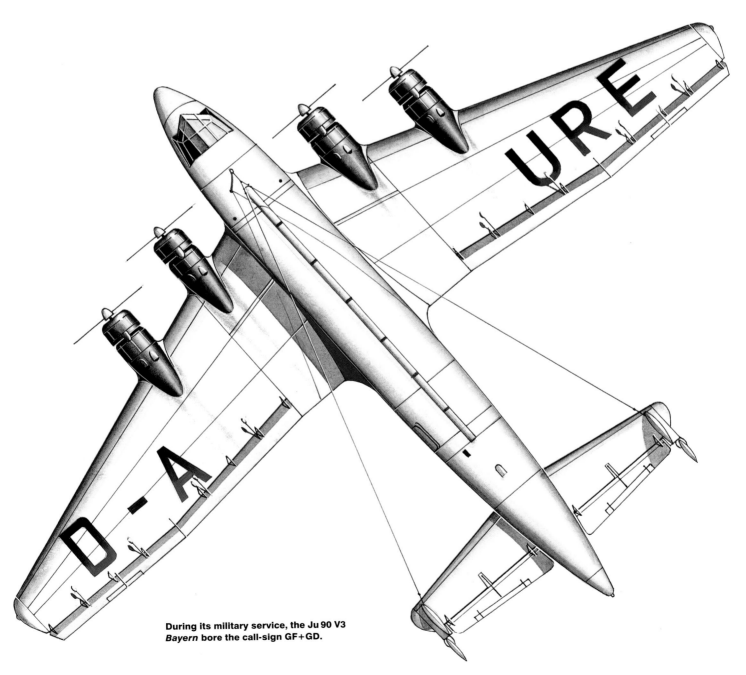

During its military service, the Ju 90 V3
Bayern **bore the call-sign GF+GD.**

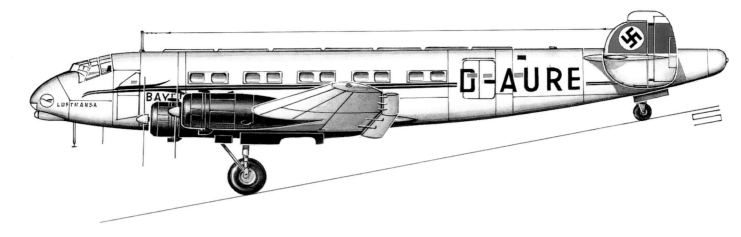

Side view of the Ju 90 V3 *Bayern*, initially named *Württemberg*.

Underside details of the Ju 90 V3.

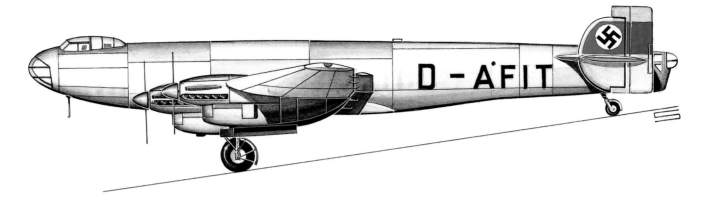

Side view of the Ju 89 V1, which had to make way for the medium bomber concept.

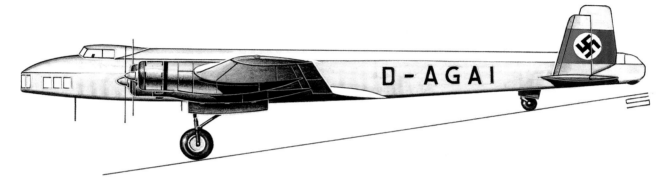

A competitor to the Ju 89 was the sole Do 19 V1 prototype.

A model photograph of the Ju 90 *Brandenburg*. This Airmodell kit is unfortunately no longer available.

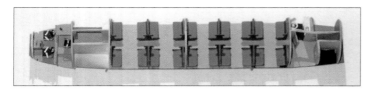

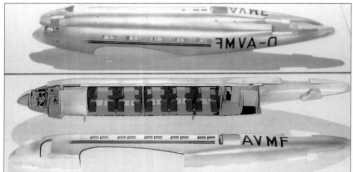

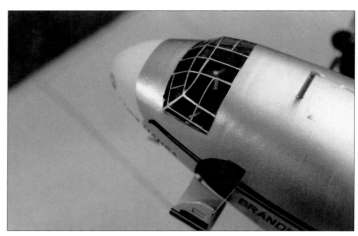

Model of the Ju 90 *Brandenburg* photographed from various perspectives.

Sources and Acknowledgements

This book is based mainly upon original documents, enabling a far more authentic account than is obtainable from secondary literature. The latter, however, were also consulted, and include the following reliable works:

Die deutsche Luftwaffe series: Bernard & Graefe Verlag
Vol 1: *Kurt Tank – Konstrukteur und Testpilot bei Focke-Wulf;* Wolfgang Wagner, 1980.
Vol 2: *Flugmotoren und Strahltriebwerke;* Gersdorff/Grasmann/Schubert, 1981.
Vol 5: *Ernst Heinkel – Pionier der Luftfahrt;* H Dieter Köhler, 1983.
Vol 9: *Typenhandbuch der deutschen Luftfahrttechnik;* Bruno Lange, 1986.
Vol 24: *Hugo Junkers – Pionier der Luftfahrt;* Wolfgang Wagner, 1996.
Vol 28: *Der deutsche Luftverkehr 1926-1945;* Karl-Dieter Seifert, 1999.

Die Grossen Dessauer: Karl Kössler and Günter Ott; Aviatic Verlag, 1993.
Flugzeugindustrie und Luftrüstung in Deutschland: Lutz Budraß; Droste Verlag, 1998.

The majority of the photographs are from the author's collection, those of various individuals mentioned below, the Lufthansa EADS Heritage, and the Publisher's archives. Written material, identified as original documents, has been taken from original Aircraft Handbooks. Transcripts of the original documents were unavoidable as their quality is unsuitable for reproduction purposes.

The author wishes to express his heartfelt thanks to all the individuals and institutions without whose kind support this book would not have been possible. Special thanks are due to Michael Baumann, Hauke Sellner, Arnd Siemon, Harald Schuhler, and Ralf Swoboda, responsible for the informative colour illustrations. No lesser thanks go to Ralf Schlüter, who completed the illustrated Ju 90 model and who compiled the accompanying construction report.

Karl-Heinz Regnat

JAGDWAFFE SERIES VOLUME ONE

Volume 1, Section 1
Birth of Luftwaffe Fighter Force
Softback , 303 x 226 mm, 96 pages
c250 photos. 0 952686 75 9 **£12.95**

Volume 1, Section 2
The Spanish Civil War
Softback, 303 x 226 mm, 96 pages
c250 photos. 0 952686 76 7 **£12.95**

Volume 1, Section 3
Blitzkrieg & Sitzkrieg 1939-40
Softback , 303 x 226 mm, 96 pages
c250 photos. 0 952686 77 5 **£12.95**

Volume 1, Section 4
Attack in the West 1940
Softback, 303 x 226 mm, 96 pages
c250 photos. 0 952686 78 3 **£12.95**

JAGDWAFFE SERIES VOLUME TWO

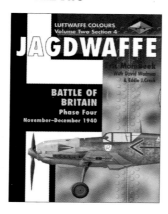

Volume 2, Section 1
BoB Phase 1: June-July 1940
Softback, 303 x 226 mm, 96 pages
c250 photos. 1 903223 05 9 **£14.95**

Volume 2, Section 2
BoB Phase 2: Aug-Sept 1940
Softback, 303 x 226 mm, 96 pages
c250 photos. 1 903223 06 7 **£14.95**

Volume 2, Section 3
BoB Phase 3: Sept-Oct 1940
Softback, 303 x 226 mm, 96 pages
c250 photos. 1 903223 07 5 **£14.95**

Volume 2, Section 4
BoB Phase 4: Oct-Dec 1940
Softback, 303 x 226 mm, 96 pages
c250 photos. 1 903223 08 3 **£14.95**

JAGDWAFFE SERIES VOLUME THREE

Volume 3, Section 1
Strike in the Balkans: April-May 1941
Softback, 303 x 226 mm, 96 pages
c250 photos. 1 903223 20 2 **£14.95**

Volume 3, Section 2
Barbarossa: Invasion of Russia April-
May 1941. Sbk, 303 x 226 mm, 96pp
c250 photos. 1 903223 21 0 **£14.95**

Volume 3, Section 3
War over the Desert: N Africa June 1940
to June 1942. Sbk, 303 x 226 mm, 96pp,
c250 photos. 1 903223 22 9 **£14.95**

Volume 3, Section 4
The War in Russia: Jan-Oct 1942
Softback, 303 x 226 mm, 96 pages
c250 photos. 1 903223 16 4 **£14.95**

JAGDWAFFE SERIES VOLUME FOUR

Volume 4, Section 1
Holding the West: 1941 to 1943
Softback, 303 x 226 mm, 96 pages,
c120 photos 1 903223 34 2 **£14.95**

Volume 4, Section 2
The Mediterranean: 1942 to 1943
Softback, 303 x 226 mm, 96 pages,
c120 photos 1 903223 35 0 **£14.95**

Volume 4, Section 3
War in Russia: Nov 1942 to Dec 1943
Softback, 303 x 226 mm, 96 pages,
c120 photos 1 903223 36 9 **£14.95**

Volume 4, Section 4
The Mediterranean: 1944 to 1945
Sbk, 303 x 226 mm, 96pp, c200 photos
1 903223 46 6 April 2004 c**£16.99**

KAMPFFLIEGER
Bombers of the Luftwaffe Volume One: 1933-1940

J R Smith and E J Creek

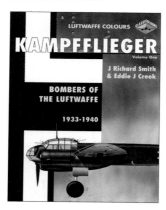

This, the first of four volumes, begins with an outline of the clandestine German bomber development following the end of World War One up to the birth of the new Luftwaffe under the Nazi Party in 1933 and the evolution of the German bomber force. The Luftaffe's debut in the Spanish Civil War and the formation of the new Kampfgeschwader is covered. Also includes the invasion of Poland, the birth of Blitzkrieg and concludes with the eve of the invasion of the West.

Softback, 303 x 226mm, 96 pages
c230 photos, 15 col profiles, maps
1 903223 42 3 **£16.95**

MESSERSCHMITT Me 163 VOLUME TWO

S Ransom & Hans-Hermann Cammann

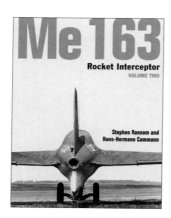

Following years of detailed research, this is the second volume in a two volume study of the Luftwaffe's legendary Messerschmitt Me 163 rocket-powered interceptor.

The authors have found incredible new documentary material and previously unpublished photographs, receiving co-operation from many former pilots who flew this radical and daunting aircraft, as well as Allied pilots who encountered it in combat.

Hardback, 303 x 226 mm, 224 pages, c300 photos, 20 colour artworks
1 903223 13 X **£35.00**

ON SPECIAL MISSIONS
The Luftwaffe's Research and Experimental Squadrons 1923-1945

J R Smith, E Creek and P Petrick

The story of the Verschuchsverband, the Trials and Research Unit of the Luftwaffe High Command, one of the most intriguing, clandestine and rarely-covered elements of the Luftwaffe before and during World War Two.

Using unpublished recollections from pilots who flew secret, long-range recce and spy-dropping missions, as well as hundreds of rare and fascinating photos, the book recounts the history, operations and aircraft of the unit.

Hardback, 303 x 226 mm, 128 pages, c360 b/w photos, 15 colour artworks
1 903223 33 4 **£19.95**

HELICOPTERS OF THE THIRD REICH

S Coates with J C Carbonel

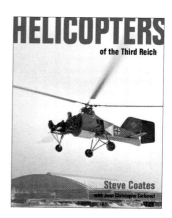

By the end of the Second World War, the Germans were, despite minimal funding and bitter inter-service rivalries, technologically ahead of their American counterparts in the development of rotating-wing aircraft. This book is the first comprehensive account of the development of auto-gyros and helicopters in Germany during 1930 to 1945 and sheds light on an unjustly neglected area of considerable aeronautical achievement.

Hardback, 303 x 226 mm, 224 pages, 470 b/w and colour photos, plus dwgs
1 903223 24 5 **£35.00**